FISHING TALK

Further details of Poppyland Publishing titles can be found at
www.poppyland.co.uk
where clicking on the 'Support and Resources' button will lead to pages specially compiled to support this title.

Copyright © 2014 David Butcher

ISBN 978 1 909796-07-2

Published by Poppyland Publishing, Cromer, Norfolk, 2014

All rights reserved. No part of this book may be reproduced, stored in a retrieval system, or transmitted in any form or by any means, electronic, mechanical, photocopying, recording or otherwise without the prior permission of the publishers.

A catalogue record for this book is available from the British Library.

Picture Credits:

J.Wells 131
Poppyland Publishing Collection 2, 22, 51, 175, 176, 180
Poppyland Photos 6, 31, 79, 103, 127, 143, 164w

Printed by Lightning Source

Overleaf: Beachmen at Lowestoft, in a photo by H.H.Tansley, early in the 20th century.

FISHING TALK

DAVID BUTCHER

In memory of George Ewart Evans and Colin Elliott

Sheringham fishermen, often called **Shannocks**, when the traditional double-ended **crab-boats** still worked from the two beaches.

Fishing Talk
The Language of a Lost Industry
drawn mainly from East Anglian sources

David Butcher

Contents

Foreword	8
Glossary of terms	11
Appendix 1: Superstition and the Fisherman	155
Appendix 2: North Sea folksongs referred to in text	165
Postscript: the sinking of the *Eta*	177
Select Bibliography	181

Foreword

The words and phrases listed in the pages which follow largely derive from the transcripts of a series of tape-recordings made between February 1976 and November 1983. Altogether, 101 hours' worth of material was collected from forty-five respondents (thirty-eight men and seven women), each of whom was connected in one way or another with the East Anglian fishing industry during the period 1910-1960. With the exception of a married couple from Peterhead and a man from Louth, all the people recorded were native East Anglians, largely living in the Lowestoft area, and they spoke in the local dialect without self-consciousness or affectation. This was a noticeable aspect of four oral histories deriving from the tapes, which were published between 1979 and 1987 (*The Driftermen*, *The Trawlermen*, *Living from the Sea* and *Following the Fishing*). The tapes themselves (BASF C60s) were gifted to the Suffolk Record Office in 2008, together with a set of transcripts, and now form part of the county's oral history collection. Another set of transcripts is lodged at the University of Freiburg, Germany, as part of its specialist, post-graduate study of English regional dialects.

A number of the terms recorded here have a general maritime application, but most relate specifically to fishing. No attempt has been made to separate the two categories, because this book represents an overall vocabulary in use when fishing was a major contributor to the East Coast economy, and to British coastal economies in general. As things stand, the national fishing industry is a pale shadow of its former self, both in terms of the vessels working and the number of people employed. The downward trend is a continuing one, with East Anglia particularly hard hit. As long ago as the summer of 2002, the Colne Fishing Company of Lowestoft (the sole survivor of about five main enterprises) ceased operating its fleet of mid-water beam trawlers – the last of these, *St. John* (LT 88) being sold to Dutch owners early in 2005.

The inability to make these boats pay their way was a combination of increasing expenses and decreasing fish stocks. It still remains to be seen whether the North Sea will recover sufficiently to provide a sustainable industry for vessels of more modest catching-capacity – especially in the light of the intensive activity carried out there and the political nature of the European debate (on the part of the nations concerned) when it comes to commercial fishing. And, in any case, the handful of fishermen and fish merchants left working in Lowestoft feel strongly that they are to be sacrificed in the cause of the port's facilities being increasingly turned over to activities connected with the renewable energy industry – particularly those associated with the Greater Gabbard Windfarm.

At the time when the people whose everyday terminology is recorded here were working, the collapse of a large-scale national fishing operation (to say nothing of its local branch) would have seemed most unlikely – if not impossible. Though, it might well be argued that the decline of the North Sea herring fishery during the 1950s and 60s stood as a warning. This book looks at all sides of the industry: the types of vessel used; the catching methods and the species sought; the means of processing catches and distributing them; and the social and economic factors affecting those employed. Account is also taken of expressions acquired in other parts of Britain (visited on a seasonal basis by East Anglian fishermen and shore-personnel as part of their working year) and of the terminology brought into East Anglia during the autumn season by visiting Scottish fishermen and herring-processors.

The author of this book (perhaps editor would be a more accurate description) is neither lexicographer nor etymologist. However, it seemed right that some attempt should be made to give the derivation of words and phrases wherever this might be useful or instructive (and where it was possible to do so), and this has accordingly been done. Many of the expressions recorded are, in any case, of obscure origin, either being slang terms of one kind or another or metaphorical in nature – the product of human response to the working environment. What the whole collection does possess is a vigour and directness that stems from people being in contact with (and sometimes opposition to) Mother Nature, in the day-to-day matter of earning a living.

No writer works in complete isolation. A debt of gratitude is obviously due to the respondents, referred to earlier, who gave generously of their time and interest to help create the tape-recorded archive. Then there were the various other people with whom incidental conversation on the subject of fishing at sea reinforced and sometimes extended the working terminology set down in this book. George Ewart Evans (who validated the use of oral history as an academic discipline in the United Kingdom with his own pioneering work on the East Anglian farm worker) was supportive of the tape-recording project from its early stages and offered both encouragement and sound advice on how to best collect the material. Colin Elliott appeared out of the blue, as the result of a chance meeting with a Lowestoft bookshop manager at an Olympia fair and thereby hearing about the work – deciding, soon afterwards, that it had the potential for readership and subsequently guiding all four titles (referred to above) to publication.

On the practical matter of scrutinising the text and bringing his own wealth of knowledge to bear, a special mention must go to Bob Malster, East Anglia's leading maritime historian, who corrected error where necessary and added further to a number of specific references with relevant and useful information. Finally, a debt is owed to Peter Stibbons of Poppyland Publishing, who has produced the book in an attractive and accessible format and made the final stages of its creation easy to bear. The selection of images chosen by him to serve as periodic illustrations is both appropriate and imaginative.

Glossary of Terms

A

Afore the wind: the term used of a vessel sailing or steaming with the wind astern. The first word derives from the Old English *onforan*, meaning "in front of".

Aft(er): astern; to the rear of a vessel. The term is probably an abbreviation of *abaft*, a Middle English word meaning "back" or "backwards", with an earlier root to be found in the Old English *æftan*, meaning "behind".

Aft-sider: a steam trawler, with the wheelhouse placed to the rear of the funnel – the usual design for the earlier vessels built. Starting during the 1890s at a length in excess of 90 feet, by c. 1910 the average steam trawler had increased in size to 100-110 feet long, by 20-22 feet in the **beam** (q.v.).

After-deck: the rear deck of a craft.

After-well: a fish compartment at the rear end of the main hold. The term *well* was a throwback to the times (from the seventeenth to the nineteenth century) when cod and some other species, caught on **handlines** (q.v.) and **longlines** (q.v.), were kept alive in flooded compartments below decks until they were landed – and it is first recorded in 1614. The county of Essex was particularly associated with *well-smacks*, in ports such as Harwich, and their mode of operation is referred to in the folksong, *Cod Banging* (see Appendix 2).

Agin (against) the law: a term used to describe unusual wind conditions, which were against both expectation and normality.

Alec: a Great Yarmouth term for a Scottish sailing drifter.

All-year boat: a vessel that managed to keep fishing all the year round – notably, in the era of steam, the **drifter-trawler** (q.v.).

Allocation: a system imposed by the government during the Second World War to make sure that fish merchants got an equitable share of the catches available from a greatly reduced national fishing operation. In each port where fishing continued, merchants were allowed a proportion of the different kinds of fish landed based on their pre-war buying levels.

Allocation officer: the man appointed in each port to make sure that the Allocation System ran properly. He was usually a fish merchant or fish salesman of long standing, who had the trust of fishermen and merchants alike.

Allotment: A weekly payment made to share fishermen (mainly those who worked on drifters) and drawn in their absence by wives or other relatives. This was added up over the weeks and deducted from the payout or **settling** (q.v.) at the end of the voyage.

Along o': the term always used by fishermen to describe which particular skippers they had served with during their time at sea. "I sailed along o' Lugs Seago" or "I wuz along o' ol' Dutch Turrell for several years" were typical of the comments made. Logic dictates that the second element of the term should have been *with* – but it was always the abbreviated form of *of*!

Altona: outport to Hamburg and the major point of reception for **klondyke herrings** (q.v.), which were exported there in large numbers not only from Lowestoft, but from herring stations around the British coast.

Annatto: a vegetable dye, deriving from the fruit of a Central American tree (*Bixa orellana*) and used to colour kippers. This was done to the make the product more eye-catching to the customer (usually by the large-scale curing companies), but did not add anything to its general quality and taste. See also, **Painted ladies.**

Answer: to respond. This term was used specifically of a vessel responding to the helmsman's touch. Thus, a man might say, "I pulled the wheel over to starboard, but she din't answer."

Arbitrator: the man – usually a fish **salesman** (q.v.) – who settled disputes on the market between the fishermen and the buyers, concerning the quality of herrings.

Arles: the money paid to Scottish curing personnel by their employers when **fixing** (q.v.) was completed. The word derives from the Latin *arr(h)a*, meaning "money given to seal a bargain or agreement", and it is also sometimes encountered as *airleas* – almost certainly a Gaelic variant from the Scottish west coast or The Hebrides. ".

Armed smacks: sailing trawlers of the First World War period, associated with the port of Lowestoft, equipped with a gun on the fore-deck to carry out anti U-boat patrols in the North Sea. At first they had some limited success in sinking German submarines, based largely on the element of surprise – but once this had been lost, enemy craft stayed out of range and outgunned them from a distance. Some people at the time even believed that their use ultimately resulted in greater losses among sailing trawlers than would otherwise have occurred. The vessels equipped with guns were four in number, to begin with, and became operational during 1915: the *Inverlyon* (LT 687), the *Glory* (LT 1027), the *G & E* (LT 649) and the *Pet* (LT 560). The *G & E* belonged to Fred Moxey, who was the man always accredited in Lowestoft with suggesting to the Naval command in the town that such craft be fitted with ordnance. See also, **Gun-smacks**.

Arse: the stern or rear section of a vessel. Such metaphorical usage is easy to understand. See also, **Screwing up**

Arse-at-it: a term used to describe a trawler losing speed while fishing and dropping back towards its gear.

Arse-down: a term used of vessel sitting low in the water astern (whether engaged in fishing or not) and usually applied to **trawling** (q.v.).

Auction: the process by which fish was (and is) sold at market. The derivation of the word is the Latin *auctio*, meaning "a public sale". During periods of heavy **landings** (q.v.), fish was sometimes sold by *Dutch auction*, whereby the salesman dropped the price from its starting-point until a purchaser was found.

B

Baccy juice: seawater stained brown (hence the reference to tobacco) by the phytoplankton *Phœcystis*. This was always interpreted as a sign of poor catches of herring, or no herring at all. See also, **Hoss-pissy water**.

Back off: to unhook fish from longlines.

Back-rope: the double rope/cord at the bottom of a drift-net. It was sometimes simply referred to as "the back".

Back-strop: a short rope or cable, which joined the door to the bridle on the Vigneron Dahl refinement of the **otter trawl** (q.v.).

Bag: the cod end of a trawl.

Bag-rope: a rope that ran from foremast to bulwark on a trawler, to stop the cod end swinging too far across the deck when the net was hoisted inboard on the **gilson** (q.v.)

Bail/bale: 1. The middle handle on a Yarmouth **swill** (q.v.) basket. As this was slightly curved, the name probably derives from the Middle English *beyle*, meaning "a hoop". 2. To make a drift-net into an improvised bag, while hauling, by pulling the head-rope upwards and across to prevent lightly meshed herrings from falling out. The derivation here is probably an analogy with the act of scooping water out of a boat.

Bait-net: a drift-net with small meshes (36-40 rows per yard), used by **longliners** (q.v.) to catch herring with which to bait the hooks.

Banging for herring: noise created on deck, by crew members of a drifter, in the belief that this would cause herring shoals to rise. Striking galley utensils against each other was a common practice.

Bankboards: an alternative form of **kid boards** (q.v.).

Bark: 1. To tan, or preserve, drift-nets against the rotting effect of seawater by soaking them in **cutch** (q.v.). The word refers to the earlier practice of using oak or ash bark solution to do this. 2. To treat sails with a mixture of horse-fat, red ochre and seawater, again in the cause of preservation and also with reference to earlier means of countering the destructive effect of salt-water.

Barmskin: an oilskin apron. The term is to be found in sixteenth and seventeenth century probate inventories, usually rendered as *bermskin*. The derivation of the first element of the word is from Old English *bearm* or *barm*, meaning "the lap", and the word *barmcloth* itself simply meant "an apron". Chaucer describes Alison, in *The Miller's Tale* (c. 1390) as wearing *a barmclooth eek as whit as morne milk*.

Barrel: the drum of a winch on board a trawler.

Bass: a natural, elastic fibre deriving from certain tropical palms and used in the manufacture of ropes – especially **tissots** (q.v.). The word derives from *bast*, the inner bark of certain trees (especially limes), which was used at one time for making fibres.

Batings: that part, on the top of a trawl net, between the square and the cod end, where a tapering-down of the meshes occurred. The origin of the term is to be found in the Middle English *bate*, meaning "to decrease" or "to diminish".

Ba(u)lk: 1. A wooden pile or post on a jetty. 2. The bar of wood on which kippers were hung to be smoked. In either case, the term has a Middle English origin, meaning "a roughly squared beam", with earlier antecedents traceable in the Old English *balc* and the Old Norse *bálkr*, meaning "a partition".

Beach (The): the community which developed below the cliff at Lowestoft during the nineteenth century, as the town expanded – particularly after the coming of the railway in 1847. It was sometimes referred to as *The Beach Village*, but never by those who lived there, who often called it **The Grit** (q.v.). After the evacuations of the Second World War, and the civic improvements which followed the end of it, The Beach dwindled in size of population and was progressively demolished throughout the 1960s. The area is now occupied by an industrial estate.

Beach Bethel: a nonconformist chapel, of no specific denomination, situated in the residential area of Lowestoft described immediately above.

Beach club: a beach company.

Beach company: an East Anglian shoreside federation in which the members (largely longshore fishermen) performed salvage operations and voluntary lifeboat work. Beach companies had their origins in the eighteenth century and reached the height of their activities during the second half of the nineteenth.

Beachmen: members of a beach company.

Beads: 1. Small wooden bobbins used on a trawl's **ground-rope** (q.v.), the analogy here with a necklace being obvious. They were usually made of elm-wood because of its toughness and water-resistance. 2. Air bubbles in seawater (often indicative of the presence of mackerel).

Beam: 1.The width of a vessel at the broadest point of the hull. 2. The wooden spar that supported the upper part of the net on the earliest type of **trawl** (q.v.). In both cases, the word derives from the Old English *bēam*, meaning "a tree". On the Lowestoft **smacks** (q.v.), the length of the *beam* varied between thirty and fifty feet, depending on the size of the vessel using it.

Beam trawl: A triangular bag-net fixed to a wooden spar on its upper side and to a ground-rope on its lower one. Use of this particular type of gear can be traced back to the late fourteenth century. See also, **Trawl**.

Bear up: to give way when crossing another vessel's bow.

Beat: to tack, or sail against the wind. The physical effort, or conflict, in this is reflected in the root word: the Old English *bēatan*, meaning "to strike".

Beat/beet: to repair broken meshes on drift-nets. Chaucer has his character, The Reeve, in the tale he told, describe the rascally miller of Trumpington thus: *Pipen he koude and fisshe, and nettes beete*. The word derives from the Old English *bētan*, meaning "to amend" and is also to be found in John Wycliffe's translation of The Bible, with reference to the calling of James and John to a life of ministry (Matthew 4. 21 and Mark 1. 19). Both uses referred to date from the late fourteenth century.

Beating/beeting-chamber: the first-floor room of a **net-store** (q.v.), long and without internal partitions, where **drift-nets** (q.v.) were laid out and repaired. Often, the term was applied to the net-store as a whole.

Beating/beeting-knife: a small shut-knife used for cutting drift-net meshes as part of the repair process.

Beating/beeting-money: the payment made to drifter crew-members for repairing nets on board during a voyage.

Beating/beeting-needle: a small hand-bobbin, made of bone or wood, used for mending drift-nets.

Beatster/beetster: a woman who repaired drift-nets.

Beatster's/beetster's hook: a double-pronged hook, fixed to a wall, on which a drift-net was hung while being mended. Women who repaired nets at home often had the hook set next to the kitchen window. At Kessingland, wooden pegs on the wall of the beating-chamber were employed instead of hooks.

Becket(t): a loop at the end of a drift-net's head-rope or back-rope.

Bed-plate: the cast-iron base, onto which a steam-reciprocating marine engine was bolted. It was also called the **sole-plate**.

Beef-kettle: a large metal pot for cooking meat and vegetables on board ship. Origins of the word may be seen in the Old English *cétel*, the Old Norse *ketill* and the Latin *catillus*.

Beef of the sea: a term used of the Cod (*Gadus morrhua*), because of its staple nature in the British fishing industry and the firm, sweet quality of its flesh. The expression was much more associated with the major trawling ports of Grimsby and Hull than with Great Yarmouth and Lowestoft.

Beekles engine: a Scottish term for a marine engine made by Elliott &

Garrood Ltd., of Beccles – particularly the renowned unit known as the **monkey triple** (q.v.). The first element, of course, results from the pronunciation given to the name of the Suffolk town from someone north of the border.

Belgian devil: a sharp-edged grapnel that was towed behind a vessel and used to sever a line of drift-nets, prior to stealing the ones that floated loose. It was a device that was sometimes used by Belgian fishermen against their English counterparts, in the North Sea, during the nineteenth and early twentieth centuries. Other variations of the term occur as *French devil* and *Dutchman's devil*. It all goes to illustrate the rivalry there was in the long-established herring fishery.

Belly: the particular area on the bottom of a trawl-net, whether beam or otter gear, between the **cod-end** (q.v.) and the **wings** (q.v.). The term is metaphorical, in the sense that it makes a comparison with the under-parts of an animal.

Bellies: see **False bellies**.

Belly-rope: an alternative name for a **lazy deckie** (q.v.).

Bend: to join two ropes by means of eyes and whippings. The word is a variant of *bind*.

Berb: the barb of a fishing-hook. The word is an example of variant pronunciation.

Berth: 1. a job on board a fishing vessel. 2. A sleeping-place on board ship. 3. The position of a vessel at sea relative to other boats engaged in fishing. 4. A vessel's place at the quayside, when moored.

Berthing master: a harbour official who showed boats where to moor and tried to control their movements when the quayside was congested.

Bethel: a non-denominational fishermen's chapel of evangelical persuasion and practice. The word derives from the Hebrew *bêt'ēl*, meaning "the house of God", the first reference being found in Genesis 28. 19, when Jacob gave the name to the place where he had had his dream of the ladder stretching from earth to heaven. There was still a Bethel in Lowestoft, opposite the fish market, at the end of the twentieth century – but it has since closed and the building is now the headquarters of the Lowestoft Players acting company.

Bethel flag: a mast-head pennant flown on vessels belonging to owners who worshipped at the Lowestoft Bethel.

Bethelite: someone who worshipped at the Bethel or was in some way connected with it.

Big Bethel: the Lowestoft non-denominational chapel, as described above. The name referred to both its physical size and the number of worshippers, as contrasted with its smaller counterpart located on **The Beach** (q.v.).

Big-boating: a term used by **longshoremen** (q.v.) for going on drifting or trawling voyages. A number of them did this during the 1920s and 30s because it sometimes offered a better means of earning a living than their usual operation, which was much more susceptible to the vagaries of the weather and the sharp practice of the lesser merchants who purchased the catches.

Bight: 1. A loop in the end of a rope. 2. A foul, or snag, in a **warp** (q.v.). The word derives from the Old English *byht*, meaning "a bend".

Bilge: 1. The bottom-most part of a ship's hull. 2. The curve of a barrel. Both meanings probably have their origin in the word *bulge*.

Billage: A variant pronunciation of *bilge*, in the first sense of the word given immediately above.

Bird's (bicycle shop): a business located at No. 2 Suffolk Road, not far from Lowestoft Fish Market. Not only did Melbourne Bird, the proprietor, sell and repair cycles, he also offered safe storage (for a small price) of fishermen's bikes while they were engaged in either the autumn herring season or trawling **voyages** (q.v.). A number of Lowestoft fishermen lived out of town, in the surrounding villages (and in ones further removed) and some of them used to cycle to their place of work both for convenience and to save the money otherwise spent on bus and train fares.

Bismarck herring: a particular kind of pickled herring, produced in Germany, which is marinated in white wine vinegar and spices. It was first produced (using Baltic herrings) in the town of Stralsund by Johann Wiechmann, who sent Otto von Bismarck a complimentary cask of the fish for his birthday and who, subsequently, in 1871, was allowed to market the product under the German Chancellor's name. After the establishment of the **Klondyke trade** (q.v.) during the 1890s, the East Anglian autumn herring season became a major source of supply.

Black-gut: discolouration of the herring's gut and surrounding flesh, caused by the plankton which constituted the feed on certain fishing grounds (notably, those off the Shetland Isles).

Blackjack: the Saithe, or Coalfish (*Pollachius virens*) – a member of the cod family, which was commonly caught on **handlines** (q.v.) by driftermen working on the summer herring voyage at Shetland and sold by them for spending-money when they docked. This species predated on herring, hence its presence among the shoals. The nickname recorded here resulted from its very dark dorsal area.

Black-noses: the East Anglian autumn herrings from the Smith's Knoll area (which were much favoured for curing into **red herrings** (q.v.). The name derives from a dark, purplish tinge on the front of the head.

Blade: a device for holding cotton skeins, prior to loading **beating-needles** (q.v.). It consisted of a wooden cross-piece, with vertical ends, which rotated on a central pillar and allowed the cotton twine to be pulled out in the lengths required.

Bladed weed: seaweed(s) belonging to the *Laminariaceae* family, especially *Laminaria digitata* (Oarweed) and *Laminaria hyperborea* (Foslie Frond).

Blakeys: protective, curved, iron studs in the soles of boots and shoes. The name is a trade brand of a company in Leeds, which began production in 1902 and still continues today. See **Appendix 1**, no. 8.

Blank: no activity on a fish market (especially where herring-trading was concerned).

Blinder: a piece of fine-meshed net fixed inside the **cod end** (q.v.) of a trawl, so as to prevent small fish from escaping. The practice continues today as a means of evading the regulations laid down concerning the minimum size of species caught and landed. The word derives from the medieval usage of the verb *blind*, meaning "to hide".

Bloater: 1. A herring lightly salted and smoked with the gut left in. As such, it was somewhat perishable and needed to be consumed within about a day of processing. This type of cure is generally reckoned to have started in Great Yarmouth during the first half of the nineteenth century – the invention of a merchant called Bishop. However, there are earlier precedents for this particular process, with the term *blown herrings* and *bloat herrings* being used to describe the product (Ben Jonson makes reference to the latter in his *Masque of Augurs*, 1622). 2. A nickname applied to any inhabitant of Great Yarmouth, by association with its most famous product. Right up until the 1960s, holidaymakers in the town were still posting specially-made, light wooden boxes containing bloaters and **kippers** (q.v.) to friends and relatives in their home areas.

Blob(s): jellyfish of any kind. The image of something globular and translucent is easy to grasp.

Block: 1. A trawler's **towing-block** (q.v.). 2. A bench-top, or table, in a fishmonger's shop, on which fish were prepared for sale.

Block-fillet: a double-sided fillet, cut across the width of the fish.

Blockman: a man who cleaned and filleted fish in a fishmonger's shop.

Block up: to secure a steam, or diesel, trawler's **warps** (q.v.), in the towing-block prior to fishing.

Bloke: a term used by Lowestoft steam-drifter crewmen to address the skipper. Eric Partridge, in *The Penguin Dictionary of Historical Slang*, notes the word as an occasional term of address among sailors.

Blondes: Blonde rays (*Raja brachyuran*).

Blood pickle: the solution of salt and herring juices which formed in the barrel after gutted herrings had been packed according to the **Scotch Cure** (q.v.) method.

Blow: a gale. The fisherman would probably speak thus: "We got caught in a real bad southerly blow!"

Blow down: 1. To let the boiler fire go out on a marine steam-engine. 2. To shout down the speaking-tube from **wheelhouse** (q.v.) or **bridge** (q.v.) to engine-room. The end of the speaking-tube was plugged with a whistle which could be used to attract attention by blowing down the tube; the whistle was removed when the tube was in use.

Blow off: the term used of safety-valves activating on steam-reciprocating engines, in order to relieve pressure on the boiler.

Blower: a whale, or porpoise (usually the former). The word takes note of the effect of the animal's air-hole as it swam along.

Bluff-bowed: the term used of a vessel, which was broad in the bow. Its derivation may be from the Dutch *blaf*, meaning "broad and flat".

Board: to transfer catches from fishing craft onto a carrier vessel, which then took the fish to Billingsgate market. Thus, the word has the conventional meaning of drawing alongside a vessel and going aboard. The operation was also known as **trunking** (q.v.), the fish being carried in large, wooden boxes called trunks.

Boat: a general term for any type of fishing vessel. The word was always pronounced with the same vowel-sound as "book" or "look".

Boat-club: a beach company. The term derives from the craft – **gigs** (q.v.) and **yawls** (q.v.) – which were used in salvage and life-saving work, as well as from the required membership of a particular fraternity engaged in such activity.

Boat-deck: the raised portion of a vessel's after-deck, where the little boat, or lifeboat, is situated.

Bobbins: wheel-like devices on an otter trawl's **ground-rope** (q.v.), facilitating ease of passage over a rough seabed.

Bogeyman: a fisheries patrol vessel, whose function was to enforce its country's limit-line, or exclusion zone. The term has a certain degree of humour to it, with its implied reference to the Devil or to some kind of malign spectre.

Bogie: a low, four-wheeled trolley, used to move boxes of fish on the quayside (especially used with reference to Lerwick, in the Shetland Isles). The word is a northern dialect one of unknown origin.

Bolch/bolsh-line: a line, or rope that was part of a beam trawl's set-up. The small bolsh ran along the top of the net behind the beam and had the meshes seized onto it. Thus, it connected the meshes to the beam. The large, or thick, bolsh performed a similar task along the **ground-rope** (q.v.).

Borsprit: a variation of **bowsprit** (q.v.).

Bosom: the curved mouth of a trawl-net in contact with the seabed.

Bosun: third in command on a steam trawler, below skipper and mate. In Lowestoft, the term **third hand** (q.v.) was used. The word derives from "boatswain", a fifteenth century term for the man in charge of a vessel's sails and rigging, which in turn has its origin in the Old English *bātsweġen*.

Bottles: spherical glass floats fixed to the head-rope of **seines** and **trawls** (q.v.). They were popular at one time as curios or decorative objects in the home and are still to be seen in antique-centres and bric-brac shops.

Bottom fish: demersal species – especially the commercial kind (e.g. cod, haddock, plaice, soles etc.)

Bow: 1. An eye in the end of a rope. 2. The rounded half-section of a Yarmouth swill basket. In each case, the pronunciation is *bō*.

Bower anchor: the anchor carried at the bow of a vessel.

Bower cable: a mooring cable attached to a bower anchor, especially as used on lightships.

Bowl: 1. A small wooden cask used as a float on drift-nets – the forerunner of the later, canvas **buff** (q.v.). 2. The curve of a fishing-hook.

Bowman: a lifeboatman (next in rank to the second cox'n) who looked after the ropes and equipment for'ad.

Bowsprit: a spar projecting from a vessel's bow, which supported stays and sails. The second element of the word derives from the Old English *sprēot*, meaning "a pole".

Boy: a term for the cook on a fishing vessel (especially a sailing smack), sometimes regardless of his age. It was customary for a youngster to start his career as cook and then work his way up the rankings, but some skippers preferred to have the services of an older, more experienced hand in the galley (at a higher rate of pay) so that the food cooked and served up was of a higher standard than that produced by a novice.

The crew of the Yarmouth sailing drifter *Our Boys*. Various parts of the rigging are clearly seen; the **bowsprit** is drawn back on board whilst in harbour. The **boy** stands at the bow of the vessel.

Braid: to make the meshes of a trawl-net. The word probably derives originally from the Old English *breġdan*, meaning "to move (the hands) to and fro".

Brand(ing): the mark burnt onto barrels of Scotch-cure herrings, to indicate top quality. This consisted of a crown, the word "Scotland" and the size category (there were seven in all) of the fish processed.

Brass on the tiller: an "in-joke" among men who worked on sailing **smacks**

(q.v.). If the tiller had decorative brass-work on it, it was reckoned that the vessel carried jam among her rations. The quality of food supplies on fishing craft generally was often the source of humour (and complaint!) among crew members – but jam was, in fact, always carried as one of the staple items to eat with bread while at sea.

Brick-dust: coarse cocoa drunk on board fishing vessels, especially that supplied by the Hull firm, Tickler & Co. The reference, in terms of both texture and taste, says a great deal! If left to simmer continuously in a container (which was the usual way of preparing it), a layer of grease eventually built up on the surface of the brew.

Brickie: 1. A Brixham-built smack. 2. A Brixham fisherman.

Bridge: the equivalent of a **wheelhouse** (q.v.) on vessels larger than those employed in fishing. It tended to be associated with naval and merchant-service craft, but also became used sometimes of the drifters and trawlers requisitioned in both world wars for patrolling and minesweeping duties – this, by process of transference from one sphere of activity to another.

Bridger (a): the term used in Lowestoft for the opening of the road bridge separating the outer and inner harbours (but also linking the northern and southern parts of the town's main commercial area), to allow vessels to enter or leave port. It is a sometimes inconvenient feature of local life which people have learned to live with over many years.

Bridle-gear: the Vigneron Dahl trawl, a French refinement of the basic otter trawl, which involved using long bridles between the doors and the net, thus giving the gear a greater "sweep" and catching capacity.

Bridles: wire guys that joined the **trawl-heads** to the **warp** (q.v.) on a **beam trawl**, or the two **doors** to the net on an **otter trawl** (q.v.).

Brill: a bad mood. The term was used especially of skippers when things on board were not going well: "The ol' man hed a right brill on."

Brine-cask/tub: a wooden barrel used on some of the steam trawlers to produce joints of salt-beef. It was usually lashed in place between the galley-door and the mizzen mast, and saltpetre (*Potassium nitrate*) was often added to the brine to increase its potency. The solution was judged to be ready for the meat when an egg-sized potato would float in it. Once the beef had had long enough in the brine, it was always cooked by boiling.

Bring up: to bring a vessel to a halt and drop anchor.

Britch(es): the female cod's roe. The name probably derives from the roe having a shape not unlike a pair of flounced *breeches*.

Broach (to): the term used when a vessel suddenly veered to windward, bringing her broadside to wind and sea.

Broadside: an expression used to describe a vessel lying beam on across the wind or tide, or both.

Brogue: a hole left in the top of tins, to exhaust air during the canning process. The word was probably a variant of *brog*, meaning to make a hole in something with an awl or boring tool.

Brown shrimp: the Common Shrimp (*Crangon vulgaris*) – which turned brown in colour, when boiled for eating. This tended to be the speciality of Lowestoft, whereas Great Yarmouth (and Gorleston) was known for the **pink shrimp** (q.v.) or Aesop Prawn. Some local longshoremen held the opinion that the demarcation-line between the two species was the sewage-outfall pipe at Corton, which was situated about halfway between the two towns.

Brull: a variant of **brill** (q.v.).

Buckling(s): ungutted herring(s) that had first been salted, then smoked at a high temperature so as to be cooked as well as cured. They were popular on the European mainland.

Buff(s): large, spherical, inflatable canvas floats used to buoy up drift-nets.

Buff-pump: the instrument used to inflate buffs.

Buff-strop: the length of rope attaching the buff to a drift-net's **head-line** (q.v.).

Buffs up your arse: the term used of drift-nets *swaling* round on the tide towards a drifter's stern.

Bug and Flea Terrace: a row of decayed eighteenth century cottages at the northern end of Pakefield Street, where the poorest members of the community lived and which were destroyed by cliff erosion during the early 1900s. The name was probably a generic one, applied to similar dwellings in other communities. An alternative term for the area was also used: **Flea and Bug Row**.

Bugs: 1. Common Bed Bugs (*Cimex lectularius*). These were a nuisance on board ship, caused by the unhygienic conditions and the irregularity with which bedding was changed. Steam and diesel trawlers seem to have been the craft worst affected, and if the infestation proved sufficiently serious Lowestoft Borough Council would fumigate any vessels upon request.

One of the writer's respondents worked on a **motor-smack** (q.v.) during the 1950s and once made the following comment: "The bloody bugs aboard her, they were enough to turn yuh out o' yuh bunk!" 2. Marine parasites of different kinds detected on fish. See also, **Lousy**.

Bulk(ing): loosely fill(ing) a barrel of Scotch-cure herrings, but with the top and bottom correctly packed with layered fish, in the approved manner. This was occasionally done by dishonest curers, in order to speed up the packing process, use fewer fish per barrel and thus make more profit. Such subterfuge tended to be short-lived!

Bull nurse: the Larger Spotted Dogfish (*Scyliorhinus stellaris*). The *nurse* element in the name refers to healing secretions in the skin, which were supposedly beneficial for cuts and abrasions.

Bulwarks: the sides of a vessel above deck level. The word derives from the Middle Dutch *bolwerk* and was originally applied to ramparts, but became mainly used of ships at the beginning of the nineteenth century.

Bunches of grapes: tangled longlines (a situation resulting from their not being laid sufficiently tightened on the seabed, thus subjecting them to being shifted around by tidal movement).

Bundle away: to cast drift-nets immediately after they had been hauled and **scudded** (q.v.), without any cleaning carried out, and allow the wind and tide to carry them away from the boat. This was done sometimes when catches were light, in order to maximise the amount of time available for fishing.

Bung-line: a Great Yarmouth term for the **net-rope** (q.v.), or **cork-line** (q.v.), on a drift-net. The word *bung* derives from the Middle Dutch *bonghe* and refers to the use of a cork as a stopper.

Bunkboard: a plank that fitted into the front of a bunk and prevented the occupant from rolling out in a heavy sea.

Bunker: 1. A coal storage area, or hold, below decks. 2. To take coal on board a steam vessel.

Bunker-hole: a circular hole in a vessel's deck, through which coal was loaded.

Bunker-lid: the metal cover that sealed either a bunker-hole or the hole in the **kid** (q.v.), through which herrings were shovelled down into the fish-hold.

Bunts: the parts of a trawl net's wings nearest to the **quarters** (q.v.). Being roughly in the middle of the net, the term may derive from a seventeenth century word for the middle of a sail.

Busky-O!: the call-out for a crew to begin hauling nets (especially on a drifter). The term derives from the Old Norse *búask*, meaning "to prepare".

Buster: a gale. The analogy made with damage caused is obvious, though the word itself derives from the Middle English *boist(er)ous*, meaning "rough in behaviour".

Butterflies: very small plaice (the smallest class/category on the Lowestoft fish market). They were popular with local fish-friers, who used them to provide a low-cost item in their shops.

Butterfly: the Ross patent **dan leno** (q.v.) in use on Vigneron Dahl trawling gear, one component of which was supposed to resemble the configuration of a butterfly's wings.

Butterfly ray: the Cuckoo Ray (*Raja naevus*). It was so called because the two roundels on the upper parts of its wings were supposed to resemble those on the wings of the Peacock butterfly (*Nymphalis io*).

Butt: 1. The Halibut (*Hippoglossus hippoglossus*) – largest of the European flatfish and referred to here in abbreviated form. 2. The Flounder (*Platichthys flesus*). The word *butt*, in this case, derives from the Middle Dutch *butte* or Danish *bot*. In the Middle Ages, it was a term applied to flatfish generally, with flounders bearing the specific title of *black butts*. Spearing these in coastal creeks and inlets was a common occupation.

Buyer: a man who purchased fish on a market, for a customer or client if an independent operator, or for an employer.

Buzzer: the Edible Sea-urchin (*Echinus esculentus*).

C

Cabin: a fishing vessel's living-quarters, below decks and usually located in the stern. There is a good reconstruction of a steam drifter's cabin in the Lowestoft and East Suffolk Maritime Museum, Whapload Road. Lowestoft – along with a hugely varied collection of pictures and artefacts relating to the local fishing industry generally.

Call out: to rouse crew members from their bunks to begin hauling nets.

Camperdown crawlers: Brittle-stars, especially *Ophiura texturata*, which were often trawled up off the Dutch coast in the particular location named. *Camperduin*, to give the place its Dutch spelling, is on the coast north-west of Alkmaar. The Battle of Camperdown was fought on 11th October, 1797, between a British fleet under Admiral Adam Duncan and a Dutch fleet under Vice-Admiral Jan de Winter. Following the battle, which resulted in a decisive defeat for the Dutch, the two opposing admirals are said to have been seen walking the streets of Great Yarmouth like two old friends.

Cant: an alternative name for **tack** (q.v.), used as both noun and verb. The origin would seem to be a mid nineteenth century usage, meaning "a deflection from the perpendicular or horizontal".

Capstan: a vertical, machine-driven or hand-powered winch, used for winding in warps on sailing smacks and herring-drifters. Arguably, the most famous model of all was the steam version made by Elliott & Garrood of Beccles, in Suffolk. Between the 1880s and 1960s, over 7,000 of these were made and fitted to fishing vessels – the first one of all being put into the Lowestoft sailing drifter *Beaconsfield* (LT 156) in 1884. The fitting of steam capstans was an expensive process, to begin with, and boat-owners customarily took out a share of their vessels' earning to meet the cost. However, even when the machinery had become a standard piece of equipment (and herring-drifters had converted from sail to steam-power), the owners still took out a share for the capstan – a practice that was cited by some fishermen as evidence of the way in which they were "ripped off".

Carlton's Dutch Drops: liquorice-based sweets for colds, sore throats and the like, made during the late nineteenth and early twentieth century. Many of the local fishermen regarded these as a universal cure-all.

Carry: a term used by **klondykers** (q.v.) to describe the suitability of herrings to stand being freighted to Altona, in Germany. As one of the writer's respondents once said, "You hed t' make sure the herrins would carry."

Carvel: the term used to describe the build of a boat, with its outer planks on the hull flush, or in line, with each other. The name derives from *caravel*, a small, fast-sailing Portuguese vessel of the sixteenth century.

Casing: the metal housing above the engine-room on a steam drifter or trawler.

Casting-bowl: a marked buff, or float, about twenty nets from the **pole-end** (q.v.) of a fleet of mackerel nets.

Cast-off: the crew member on board a drifter, who was responsible for removing the seizings from the warp during hauling. The job was one stage up from being cook and was therefore usually done by one of the younger men, though older hands sometimes performed the task as well.

Castle boats: steam trawlers belonging to the Consolidated Fishing Company Ltd. of Grimsby, which were based in Swansea and which were all named after Welsh castles – e.g. *Powis Castle* (SA 68). See also, **Crown boats**.

Catcher: a **didall** (q.v.), or some device made of net, to catch herring falling from the meshes during hauling. In the days of **rough-nets** (q.v.) made from hemp and used by sailing drifters, the fish often tended to fall from the nets as they was hauled because the meshes were less retentive than those made of cotton.

Catfish: the Wolf-fish (*Anarhichas lupus*), a formidable predator which lives on crabs, sea-urchins, molluscs etc. The bite of the larger specimens, aided by dislocation of the lower jaw, is so powerful that accounts are heard of them snapping the handles of deck-brooms. A good quality leather-substitute can be made from the skin.

Cauliflower: to top up quarter-cran baskets when landing herrings. The fishermen were often required to do this by the purchaser of the catch, to make sure that he got his due (or even more). The fishermen themselves would often try to keep the baskets no more than level full, in order to increase the total number of baskets – and, therefore, the **crannage** (q.v.) – landed. The term is a metaphorical one, whereby a well-filled basket of herrings represented the nicely rounded shape of a prime cauliflower.

Cement wash: a lime substance used to wash and cleanse drinking-water tanks on board fishing-vessels.

Chafer: a badly worn oilskin, used only in fine weather. It was so called because the neck and cuffs would cause discomfort in cold, wet conditions.

Chafing-pieces: another term for **false bellies** (q.v.).

Chance: occasional. The use of this word was always as an adjective (e.g. "Time was when you got a chance fishin' for herrins in the spring o' the year.").

Chance-time: occasionally; now and again.

Charges: a fishing-vessel's expenses for fuel, provisions, other consumable items and sales commission, which were always deducted from the boat's earnings before the crew members were paid at the end of a **trip** (q.v.) or **voyage** (q.v.).

The gear constituted a discrete item and its cost was allowed for separately – though, in the case of herring-fishing, a vessel's owner would have a share for the nets incorporated in his (or her) own entitlement.

Chase: the term used of driving the price of fish up at auction (wherever Dutch auction was not practised), in order to keep an outsider from buying or, at least, to ensure that he purchased expensively. See, also **Run**.

Chat(s): 1. Small fish (especially haddock). The term was applied during the middle of the nineteenth century to small, inferior potatoes. 2. Headlice. Again, the reference to size may be a reason for the usage.

Check-rope: a rope used to stop a beam trawl's **warp** (q.v.), from running out any further.

Cheese: a curved piece of hard wood, grooved down the middle to take the keel, which was used to enable a lifeboat (or any other vessel) to move from **score** (q.v.) to beach when being launched.

Chicken(s): small Turbot (*Scophthalmus maximus*). The expression probably refers to both age and succulent eating-quality.

Chief: the engineer on a steam/diesel drifter or trawler (especially the latter). The term is simply an abbreviation of *chief engineer*, as used in both the Royal and Merchant navies.

Chipper: a tool used for de-scaling boilers.

Chitlins: part of the male cod roe. The term refers to a supposed resemblance to a pig's *peritoneum*.

Chittled: a term used of drift-nets when the **lint** (q.v.) rolled up around the head-rope. Again, there may be a reference to pigs' intestines here, in that a chittled net might be supposed to have resembled twisted guts.

Cho(o)ker: a piece of wood used to prevent an anchor chain from running out any further, by being thrust into one of the links on the inward side of the **hawse-pipe** (q.v.). The derivation is from the middle of the eighteenth century, probably, when *choke* had the meaning (among others) of "to jam in".

Chopper: a hand-axe. Most fishing craft had at least one of these among the tools carried on board. It was used for cutting through ropes, if and when necessary, and for chipping away ice from the rigging in extreme weather conditions.

Chow(ing): tow(ing) a trawl against the tide. The term was used with regard to steam trawlers and may be onomatopoeiac in attempting to represent the sound of the engine working hard to maintain speed.

Chuck up: an expression used for a herring buyer refusing to purchase a catch after accepting the **sample**. This was done by finding fault with the main bulk, in the hope of forcing the price down. A notable exponent of the art (if it may so be termed) on the Lowestoft fish market, during the 1920s and 30s, was a certain Mr. Tucker. His trading methods led to the sobriquet, "Steve Tucker, the champion chucker".

Clean-swept: the term used of a sailing vessel losing most of its sails and rigging in a fierce gale.

Clean voyage: a term usually applied to the Newlyn mackerel fishing, because (in contrast to herring-catching) there was very little mess resulting from fish-scales.

Cleat: a shaped wooden (and, later, a steel) bar fixed to masts and gunwales and used to secure ropes.

Click: a clique. The word is a straightforward variant pronunciation.

Clinker: the term used to describe the build of a boat, with its outer planks on the hull overlapping each other from the top downwards and secured by *clinched* (or *clenched*) nails, the outwards ends of which were flattened over. The word may be compared with the Dutch *klinken*, meaning "a rivet". In this style of building, the strakes or planks were set up first and the frames then inserted.

Clinker grounds: parts of the seabed (especially in the North Sea) littered with furnace waste jettisoned by steam vessels – this being put into buckets, drawn up the engine-room ventilator shafts and thrown overboard. Such dumping-areas made trawling difficult. (See **Dirt-track** also). The term *clinker* here derives from the Dutch *klinken*, meaning "to ring". The word was originally applied to highly-fired bricks, made in the sixteenth and seventeenth centuries for paving, which made a ringing sound when struck together. Later, it came to mean a mass of bricks fused together by excessive heat, and from there it became applied to slag.

Clip: a word used to describe the way that mackerel gills were disengaged from drift-nets by being flicked out with thumb and forefinger.

Clip-link: a linking ring on the end of an otter trawl's warp, into which the **bridle** (q.v.) fitted.

Close (the): dusk. Used in this sense, to denote the closing of the day, the term has seventeenth century antecedents.

Close(s) in: become(s) dusk, or dark.

Clumpers: stout leather boots, mid-calf in length, worn by fish-market workers. The word would seem to derive from late nineteenth century usage, when

The **clinker** built hull of the *Alfred Corry* lifeboat in her museum at Southwold. Behind the rope is the bow **fender**,

clump had, as one of its meanings, a thick sole added to the one already on a boot or shoe.

Coal wherry: a shallow-draught barge which was used, in Lowestoft and Great Yarmouth, for supplying fuel to steam vessels as they lay in harbour. It was usually **quanted** (q.v.) around the moorings. The wherry proper was the classic, single-sail, trading craft of the Norfolk Broads and associated river-systems.

Coalie/Coley: an abbreviated form of Coalfish (*Pollachius virens*), a member of the cod group. The latter spelling was even adopted by the fishmongers at one time as a brand-name in their shops.

Coamings: boards which formed a protective barrier against water around the top of the fish-hold, and onto which the hatch covers fitted.

Cob(s): the hard roe(s) of female herrings.

Cob herrings: the East Anglian autumn herrings. The first element of the term might possibly have had its origins in the word sometimes being used to suggest something being rounded and stout. The autumn herring were indeed well-fleshed and of good size.

Cob mands/maunds: baskets into which split herrings were put, prior to the smoking process which turned them into **kippers** (q.v.). Both words are the names of particular types of basket, a *cob* being a small one to carry on the arm and a *mand* or *maund* being a taller, free-standing one. The word *maund* is Anglo-Saxon, but it could have been introduced into the East Anglian from the Dutch; the local pronunciation *maand* is very close to modern Dutch or Flemish.

Coble: a stout, broad-beamed beach boat used for fishing (especially that associated with the Yorkshire coast). One particular feature of its build was the high-lift stern, which was intended to diminish the effect of a **following sea** (q.v.) when the vessel was being beached. Cobles very similar to the Yorkshire version were also used during the nineteenth century on the Norfolk coast.

Cock mackerel: a half-grown mackerel.

Cod chaps: large holes, or tears, in a drift-net's meshes. The analogy here is with a cod's mouth which, when open, is of some considerable size.

Cod chaps/cheeks: the fleshy sides of a cod's head (specifically, at the back of the mouth and eyes), which were valued as food – especially in poor families.

Cod-end: the far, narrow end of a **trawl-net** (q.v.) which contains the bulk of the catch. *Cod(d)* was an Old English word for a bag.

Cod farm: an area where fish (largely the species mentioned) were laid out to dry on wooden racks, in the open air, prior to export to Mediterranean countries as *stockfish*.

Cod-line: the rope which opened, and closed, the **cod-end** (q.v.) of a trawl-net.

Cod shoulders: the area to the back of a cod's head (in front of the first dorsal fin), which was valued as food – again, largely in poor families.

Cod's head: this part of the fish was usually discarded, especially after filleting became established practice – but it was once purchased for small sums in fishmongers' shops, or scavenged off the market, to make a meal. Any flesh left on was cut off and variously used, while the head itself was sometimes cooked by boiling to make the basis of a stew.

Coil: to stow the warp of a drifter, or smack, in the **rope-room** (q.v.). This had to be done precisely and neatly, so that there would be no fouling the next time the nets were *shot*.

Combination fishing-line: strands of wire and rope twisted together into a single cable.

Come down: a term used to describe a mist or fog developing at sea.

Come fast: the term used of a trawler fouling its gear on an underwater obstruction.

Coming-in (the): daybreak.

Coming-out (the): sunset, dusk.

Companion boards: lengths of timber used to seal off the companion-way against stormy weather.

Companion-way: the stairway to and from the cabin.

Compo: compensation money. The term usually related to insurance pay-outs for damage to, or loss of, fishing-gear.

Compound: a two-cylinder steam engine, having a high-pressure cylinder from which steam was exhausted to the low-pressure cylinder.

Concrete (The): a term used by Fleetwood men (and by the Lowestoftians who migrated there during the 1930s) for a fishing-ground in the Irish Sea, where chalk or limestone outcropped on the seabed. This area was located about 20 miles south-east of the Calf of Chicken Rock (Isle of Man) and yielded good catches of hake during the summer months.

Condensed milk: before refrigeration for food on board ship was introduced, fresh milk could not easily be stored or used. Nearly all fishing-craft, therefore, carried tins of condensed milk among the provisions for putting in tea or cocoa. The number taken by a trawler to last the trip was a common means, on the part of the crew, of assessing the skipper's value. If there was sufficient condensed milk, then he was not trying to minimise the food-bill and was worth sailing with. Some masters tried to keep food-costs down (as they had to pay for what they consumed out of their wages), while others recognised that a well-fed crew would have a higher level of morale and work all the better for it.

Contraband: bonded liquor and tobacco. Such merchandise was obviously referred to in this way simply because it was what was most commonly smuggled. A favourite place to conceal spirits and tobacco products, if brought across the North Sea from Holland or Belgium, was in a steam drifter's mizzen sail furled on its **gaff** (q.v.). Not only was this an apparently unlikely place to stache smuggled goods of any kind, the sail itself was usually heavily impregnated with soot collected (when it was set) from the engine-room's funnel and therefore very messy to investigate.

Control price: A stipulated minimum/maximum sales price for fish at market. The term was particularly applied to the regulation price for herring, introduced by the government during the 1930s, in order to bring stability at a time of widely fluctuating catches and prices.

Controlled fishing: government regulation of the East Coast herring fishery during the 1930s, which limited the number of drifters fishing at any one time. This was done in the attempt to bring some sort of balance to the industry during a period of instability.

Convoy fishing: the system used during the Second World War to maintain a fishery in Icelandic waters. Trawlers based in Fleetwood (the main centre of British fishing during the war) would operate in groups of ten to twelve vessels under the command of two, large, armed craft (also trawlers), each of which carried a twelve-pounder gun, an Oerlikon and two machine guns. The smaller craft in the convoy all had a twelve-pounder, mounted on either the fore or after-decks.

Cooking: a joint of meat (a term used mainly on board ship).

Cooper: a barrel-maker. The word derives from the Middle Dutch *kūper*, meaning "a maker of tubs or vats".

Cooper's rusks: hard-tack biscuits. There are two commonly held views regarding the origin of the term. One is that it derives from Cooper & Co., one of the main marine provisioners in Lowestoft. The other says that the biscuits were so hard that they resembled barrel-staves! In 1871 Lewis B.

Cooper, of Mariner's Street, Lowestoft, introduced to his bakery machines worked by steam power for the production of ship's biscuits. A report in the *Suffolk Mercury* states that "The flour and the requisite liquor are put into an iron drum, inside of which also are iron arms termed 'kneaders'. The drum is revolved by steam power...the dough is placed on another machine, and worked through two rollers into the requisite thickness, and a set of moulds fall on to it cutting the biscuits clean out and marking them as required by the maker." See also, **Twenty-five holers**.

Coper: a Dutch "grog ship", which supplied low-grade gin and other spirits to fishermen working in the North Sea. There were a considerable number of these at one time, during the mid/late nineteenth century, supplying the great trawling fleets which worked the Dogger Bank. It was to counter their malign influence that the Royal National Mission to Deep Sea Fishermen was founded in 1881. The word *coper* derives from the Dutch *kooper*, meaning "to buy or trade".

Cork-line/cork-rope: the head-rope on a drift-net, so called because of the corks norselled in (see **Norsel**) along its length at regular intervals.

Corkscrew rope: a rope with a wire core.

Cotton: a slang term used by lifeboatmen for the rope or line which secured a stricken vessel in salvage work. See also, **String**.

Country boys: men from the inland villages who went fishing out of Lowestoft or Great Yarmouth. Originally, many of them were farmworkers who provided crew members for the expanding herring industry during the second half of the nineteenth century, taking advantage of a slack period on the land (after the harvest and autumn ploughing) to earn money in a completely different working environment. The link with herring-fishing continued after the increasing adoption of steam-power by fishing craft after c. 1900 and a number of the men then became full-time hands. Some of them (always a lesser number) also found employment on board trawlers. Though the great majority of country fishermen lived comparatively close at hand to either port, some of them travelled considerable distances to and from their work (usually by rail) – the furthest recorded by the writer being a man who worked out of Lowestoft during the 1920s and 30s, and who lived at Tunstall, in Suffolk – a distance of 25 miles or more.

Court: a beach company shed, or a meeting-room inside. In a sense, the word elevates or grandifies the building, but it may also take account of the importance of the salvage work done by beachmen and of the inquiries into wreck that sometimes took place in their headquarters.

Cover: a **blinder** (q.v.). The idea of concealment (especially if using illegal mesh sizes) is obvious.

Crab(b): a small capstan set on the beach and used for hauling longshore boats from the water.

Crab-boat: 1. the lowest money-earner among a company's fleet of fishing-vessels (especially when related to steam drifters). The analogy is, of course, with the crustacean's proverbial lack of speed. See also, **White-elephants.** 2. A North Norfolk term for a longshore craft mainly engaged in the catching of crabs, by setting **pots** (q.v.).

Crabber: A Fleetwood term for a **mid-water** (q.v.) trawler.

Cran: the official measure of herrings (established by Act of Parliament in 1908): 37½ Imperial gallons by volume or 28 stones by weight. The word derives from the Scottish (Gaelic) *craun*, meaning "a barrel".

Cran out: to unload herrings from a steam drifter in quarter-cran baskets.

Crannage: 1. The total number of crans in an individual drifter's catch. 2. The total number of crans purchased in a day by a fish merchant or curer.

Cranner: a Scotch curer's workman (sometimes a cooper by trade), who performed various tasks on the pickling plots.

Cranning-pole: the boom on a steam-drifter's foremast, which was used as a derrick (in tandem with the pulley-wheel on the side of the capstan) when landing baskets of herring in dock.

Crawlers: Brittle-stars (especially *Ophiothrix fragilis*).

Creepers: three or four-clawed grapnels.

Creosote-and-sugar: a favourite fisherman's remedy for sore throats. A sugar lump was impregnated with creosote, then placed in the mouth and allowed to dissolve. Sometimes, *Sloanes Liniment* was used as an alternative to creosote.

Crick (The): an inlet on the southern shore of Lake Lothing (Lowestoft's inner harbour), where out-of-use fishing vessels were moored until required, or sold. The word is obviously a corruption of *creek*. During the 1920s and 30s, the Consolidated Fishing Company Ltd. used this area of water to **lay up** (q.v.) vessels held in reserve. If one of its trawlers failed to earn an average £13 10s 0d a day over the length of a trip (usually eight to ten days), during the period February-April, when trawling slackened off, the crew were laid off and the vessel taken up to *The Crick*. She was replaced by one of the craft moored there, which was then taken down to the trawl dock and a fresh crew shipped on board. There was no shortage of labour in Lowestoft during the 1930s!

Crimp: to skin, bone and curl a haddock, as a way of presenting the fish for sale in a shop window.

Croc(k): a type of universal spanner, with serrated jaws, used for various tasks on board ship. The analogy with a *crocodile* is obvious.

Croom: a crome (pronounced *krum*). The word was applied specifically to a *grapnel*.

Cross-fillet: a **block-fillet** (q.v.).

Crotch-boots: a fisherman's long, leather sea-boots, reaching to the top of the thigh.

Crown boats/Crownies: steam trawlers belonging to the Consolidated Fishing Company Ltd. of Grimsby. They were given this name because the firm used a crown as its identifying motif, or badge, and this was painted on the funnel of every vessel. During the 1920s, the company moved a number of its older vessels down to Lowestoft, until the fleet numbered about thirty. All of these craft were long past their best (having been built during the 1890s) and no longer suitable for fishing the Dogger Bank and more challenging distant-water grounds, but they were capable of making profitable trips from the grounds between their new home-port and the Dutch coast, or even from running down occasionally to the Frisian Islands.

Crown-branding: another term for the Scottish Fishery Board's seal of approval on barrels of pickled herrings. See also, **Branding**.

Crow's foot: the term used for two strands of a drift-net's mesh being broken.

Crow's nests: accretions of furnace clinker on a boiler's tubes, in a steam engine.

Cucumber(s): a name given to the Smelt (*Osmerus eperlanus*), because this fish does indeed have the odour of cucumber. During the pre-industrial period, there was quite an important **draw-net** (q.v.) fishery for the species along the east coast of England, during the spring months (April and May), as it entered estuaries to spawn. In some locations, the practice lasted well into the twentieth century.

Cuddy: a term sometimes found loosely applied to foc'sle accommodation on trawlers and drifter-trawlers; a bow cupboard on smaller vessels. It probably derives from the Dutch *kaiuyte*, meaning "a shack" or "a shanty".

Culch: dross or refuse of some kind. The word was applied to fish waste, especially the herring scales which used to accumulate in the **dead well** (q.v.). It is of unknown origin and is first recorded in the 1660s.

Curl: a way of preparing skinned and gutted whiting for sale in a fishmonger's shop by inserting the tail through the eye-sockets.

Curly weed rash: an irritation to the hands (particularly those of trawlermen) caused by certain kinds of *sea chervils*. See also, **Dogger Bank itch**.

Cut your cloth: to adjust the sail area of a vessel according to weather conditions.

Cutch: the resin of the Far Eastern tree *Acacia catechu*, which was used as a preservative of drift-nets against the rotting effect of seawater.

Cutch-worm: the polychaete, *Potomilla reniformis* – a marine worm eaten by cod and other species and referred to by the term recorded because of its colour (orangey-brown) roughly resembling that of the preservative agent recorded immediately above.

Cutter: a fast-moving sailing vessel or steamboat, used for transporting catches directly from the fishing-grounds to port and, in the days of the Dogger Bank trawling fleets, to Billingsgate Market. The original use of the word referred to a fast, single-masted vessel, of gaff rig, used by the Revenue service.

D

Dabble: a trial fishing, whether drifting or trawling, to assess the catch-potential.

Daddy: a good fishing craft; a favourite boat. The word was often used by skippers of vessels they had commanded. This term of endearment for a male parent can easily be understood in this particular context – even though ships of all kinds are traditionally given female gender!

Dan: a type of buoy used by trawlers and longliners, to mark the area being fished by the former and to show the exact position of the lines by the latter. It consisted of a pole on the floating section, bearing a flag by day and a lamp at night. Drifters also used the device to indicate the furthest end from the vessel of its **fleet** (q.v.) of nets. The word can be traced back to the late seventeenth century and is sometimes found rendered as *dahn*.

Dan Leno: a device that keeps the head-rope and foot-rope apart on an **otter trawl** (q.v.), before leading down to the bridle. The original word for this pair of wooden, or iron, posts was the French *guindineaux*. On adopting this refinement during the 1920s, as part of the improved Vigneron Dahl gear, English fishermen corrupted the word to *Dan Leno*, a popular music hall performer of the late Victorian period.

Dan tow: the cord that secured the dan buoy to the seabed anchor on **longlines** (q.v.).

Dandy: a ketch-rigged sailing drifter.

Dandy/dandy bridle: the wire line, or cable, used to lift the trawl **beam** (q.v.) inboard when hauling was in progress.

Dandy-wink: the small winch mounted aft on smacks, which hauled in the trawl beam by means of the dandy bridle. *Wink* is obviously a corruption of "winch".

Dangles: metal rings linked to lengths of chain, which were fixed to the ground-ropes of trawls to help keep the gear down on the seabed and to cause the **sanding-up** (q.v.) process that was so necessary for the effective catching of flatfish.

Danish seine: a type of **mid-water trawl** (q.v.) that was paid out from a vessel pursuing a triangular course. When **shooting** (q.v.) was complete, the boat anchored and pulled the net in. This method of fishing was invented in Denmark and was popular with Lowestoft fishermen during the 1920s as a means of catching haddock on the Dogger Bank.

Day-book: a ledger in which a fish salesman's daily transactions were recorded.

Daylight swimmers: a term used for herrings that rose from the seabed at dawn (the shoals usually rose at dusk).

Dead men's fingers: 1. The part of a crab (the lungs) which, by their shape and grey colour are supposed to resemble the fingers of a corpse. They may retain toxins and are removed for cooking. 2. A colonial Bryozoan of the Alcyonacea order (soft corals): specifically, *Alcyonium digitatum*, which was often responsible for the allergenic rash known as **Dogger Bank itch**.

Dead tides: slack, low-running tides.

Dead well: a bilge space on the aft side of steam drifter's fish-hold in which herring waste (largely scales) collected after washing-down had been carried out.

Dead wind: no wind at all (a term largely used by *smacksmen*).

Deck crowd/people: the crew members of a fishing-vessel other than the skipper, mate, engineer and cook. The term is largely analogous with *deckhands*.

Deckhand: an ordinary crew member aboard a steam or diesel trawler.

Deckhand dandies: The term used for young Lowestoft trawlermen during the late 1950s and early 1960s, because of their **go-ashores** (q.v.). They wore flamboyant, brightly-coloured suits of shiny material, which had contrasting coloured lapels and cuffs on the pleated jackets (e.g. blue against red, black against green) and either bell-bottomed or drainpipe trousers. Measurements and orders were taken at *Lawrence Green* gentleman's outfitters, on Lowestoft High Street, and the clothes then made up in Leeds.

Deckie: a deckhand.

Deckie-learner: the term used in Lowestoft (and other British trawling ports), in the decades following the Second World War, for a youngster starting a career in fishing. During this period, the Lowestoft College of Further Education ran a dedicated course for boys with such intentions in an annexe on Herring Fishery Score, close to Christchurch – the Anglican place of worship built in 1868 to serve **The Beach** (q.v.) community.

Deckie-second: the term used on the **motor-smacks** (q.v.) for the man who served as both deckhand and second engineer – the other crew members being skipper, mate, third hand, chief engineer and cook.

Deep: a term used of a vessel floating low in the water. For example, "She wuz a big ol' boat an' she used t' sit deep."

Denes: open, undulating areas of grass and scrub close to the sea. The word is a variant of *dunes* and may thus be compared with the Dutch *duin*, meaning "a sandhill". The original, root word is probably the Old English *dūn* – "a hill". There are extensive denes at Lowestoft and its neighbour to the north, Gunton, and also at Great Yarmouth.

Dennies: tins of fish and fish roes that had failed the canning process and were thus rejected.

Derby day: the day on which driftermen's wives drew their husbands' **allotment** (q.v.) money at the company offices on Lowestoft fish market while a voyage was in progress (Friday). The term jokingly compares the number of people (the women would often be accompanied by young children) to that which gathered at Epsom race-course for the greatest flat event in the calendar.

Derrick: a crane with a movable boom (specifically, a steam drifter's foremast). The word derives from the surname of a Tyburn executioner during the late sixteenth and early seventeenth century (Thomas Derrick), who refined the gallows mechanism and reputedly despatched more than 3,000 people. The connection with hanging is thus easy to see.

DF: a radio-wave *direction-finder* (hence the initials). Equipment of this kind began to be fitted into the larger steam trawlers (especially in distant-water ports) during the late 1920s, to improve efficiency of navigation. Some skippers also used it to home in on vessels fishing profitably, if information of their success had been divulged on the air-waves. The initials recorded here also functioned as a verb and fishermen would refer to "d-effing" as a means of describing use of the equipment.

Dibs: money – a slang term dating back to the early nineteenth century. The word had previously been applied to small, flat, rounded stones used in the game of *five-stones* and to counters used in certain card-games. The shape of such things being transferred to coins is not hard to envisage.

Didall/didle: a tapering net on a long pole (not unlike a butterfly net, in principle), which was used to catch herrings that fell from the meshes during hauling. It was the chief engineer who usually operated the didall and the fish taken were customarily treated as an extra to be added to his wages. The usage here must have derived from the ladelling action employed, which was seen as being comparable with that of the wooden didall, or dished *shovel*, used to clean out ditches.

Diet hours: meal-breaks (a Scottish term used in connection with work on the pickling-plots).

Digby: the Herring (*Clupea harengus*) – a term particularly associated with Lowestoft and Great Yarmouth, and of unknown origin. It certainly has nothing to do with the Old English *dic*, meaning "a ditch", and the Old Norse *býr*, meaning "a settlement" or "a village".

Digging her snout in: an expression used to describe steam or diesel craft making way against wind and tide, and meeting the waves head on – thus, evocatively conjuring up an image of the vessel's **pitch** (q.v.).

Dill: the sump beneath a marine engine.

Dirt-track: a term with the same meaning as **clinker grounds** (q.v.).

Dirty: the term commonly used of a vessel which rolled a lot and thus shipped water. See **Slushy**, also.

Dirty fish: 1. A fish that was regarded as being unwholesome to eat. 2. A fish whose diet led to its gut being exceptionally mucky or discoloured in any way. In the case of the mackerel, the latter characteristic created the belief among some fishermen in the Lowestoft-Great Yarmouth area that the species was best not eaten – especially during the summer months. These same men usually had a completely different view of the mackerel caught on the Newlyn voyage during the early months of the year. These were seen as being wholesome and well-flavoured – a different species, almost!

Distant-water boat: a trawler which fished the areas specified immediately below.

Distant waters: the term used for fishing grounds off Faeroe, Iceland, Greenland etc., or in the White Sea and Barents Sea. Vessels from Fleetwood, Grimsby and Hull traditionally worked these, not craft from Lowestoft and Great Yarmouth, and they were away from home for weeks at a time.

Ditty-box: a small wooden box, used to carry a fisherman's personal effects on board – the exact equivalent of a sailor's *ditty-bag*.

Dock: 1. A large metal tank in which osiers were steeped prior to being used to make baskets. The idea behind the term, presumably, is that of a dock for ships – an area of water walled off and self-contained. 2. To cut the wings from rays and skate. The derivation here is from the word used to describe the cutting-off of animals' tails.

Docks: the bodies of rays and skate from which the wings had been cut.

Dockside dandies: an alternative term for **deckhand dandies** (q.v.).

Dodge: to keep a vessel head to wind in stormy conditions and thus avoid the worst effects of the weather. The use of the word is interesting, in that no movement to either port or starboard was involved.

Dodger: a canvas shelter under which a smack's helmsman stood in bad weather.

Dog: a dogfish; especially the Spur-dog (*Squalus acanthias*).

Dog-bin: the gut-truck, a railway wagon which took fish waste away from the market each day for industrial processing into manure.

Dog-eaten: 1. Herrings which had been damaged by dogfish (notably, the Spur-dog) while hanging in the meshes of drift-nets. A lump would be bitten out of their backs, rendering them unsaleable. 2. Drift-nets which had been torn by the spines on the Spur-dog's two dorsal fins (hence, the creature's name).

Dogger (The): the term customarily used (and pronounced "Dorgger") when referring to the *Dogger Bank*, the main trawling-area of the southern North Sea off the coast of Yorkshire, which had once formed the so-called "land-bridge" joining England to the European continental land-mass. Productive fishing was to be had over much of its total area, especially along the drowned river-valleys. See also, **Mud gulleys**.

Dogger Bank itch: curly weed rash caused by the soft coral, *Alcyonium digitatum* – a weed-like colonial animal. This affected fishermen's hands and was a notifiable industrial disease. See also, **Curly weed rash**.

Dole (on the): Being out of work and drawing unemployment pay.

Dollop: 1. A catch, or quantity, of herrings. 2. A heavy wave (used especially to describe one striking a vessel broadside on). The word may have its origin in the Norwegian dialect term *dolp*, meaning "a lump".

Dolphins: free-standing, wooden mooring-posts in a harbour.

Dome-top: a rounded metal cover above a ventilator in the deck of a sailing smack, often located near the companion-way.

Don: a top skipper; one of the biggest money-earners in a port. The term would seem to derive from the title given to a Spanish grandee and it was in particular use in Lowestoft during the 1950s and 60s.

Donkey: a subsidiary part of a marine steam engine, which worked the pumps. The analogy with a working animal is obvious.

Donkey's breakfasts: sacks filled with straw, which served as palliasses in fishing vessels' bunks. These were either prepared at the beginning of a voyage by individual crew members, or purchased from one of the local ships' stores, and they had to last for its duration. They tended to make ideal accommodation for bed bugs and fleas.

Doones: denes, or dunes.

Doors: the heavy otter boards on the upper extremities of a trawl of that name, which served as paravanes, to spread the mouth of the net while fishing was in progress.

Dootch (the): Dutch fishermen and fish-traders. The pronunciation owes something to continental influence.

Dopper: a fisherman's long slop, made of calico (and, occasionally, of oilskin) and reaching to below the knee. Because of the garment's getting frequently wet, the name may derive from *didapper*, an old name for the Dabchick, or Little Grebe (*Tachybaptus ruficollis*), a common British water bird.

Doss-house (The): a common lodging-house that stood in the old part of Lowestoft town, on the south side of St. Margaret's Plain. The term was in general use nationally from the middle of the nineteenth century until about the middle of the twentieth – by which time the social conditions that had generated the need for such cheap accommodation had changed. The first element of the term possibly derives from the Latin *dorsum*, meaning "the back" – and the idea formed of lying down and sleeping led to the word becoming a slang term for a bed during the late eighteenth century.

Double figure-eight: the knot that secured the tie around a drift-net at the end of a voyage and indicated to net-store staff that it was badly damaged.

Double-nets: the term used of extra-long sprat nets (sixty yards, instead of the usual thirty) which were produced at one time, but which never really became established because they proved unwieldy to use.

Double swum: a term used when herrings were enmeshed on either side of the nets – the result of the latter being out in the water for two tides or more. This made hauling difficult and extended the time spent doing it.

Double-talk: a type of "in-talk" employed by members of the Lowestoft beach companies, which worked on the principle of word-order reversal and was intended to obscure the meaning of what was being said when people from outside their circle were present. It was similar in principle to *back-slang*, where the letters of the words themselves are reversed in order (e.g. money becomes *yenom*).

Dover sole: the Sole (*Solea solea*). This fish was taken in trawls and seines all round the coasts of Britain, but gained the name recorded here because catches made off the coast of Kent often found their way to London. This traffic accelerated after the development of the railways and "Dover sole" became a favoured item on menus in the capital. This was not only because of the excellence of the flesh, but also because the name had a cachet of its own, suggesting as it did something utterly English.

Down: northwards. This was an expression used of the North Sea, based on the fact that the ebb tide runs in a northerly direction. Hence, when the East Anglian fishermen left home for the summer herring voyage in Scotland, they always "went down to Shetland."

Drag: 1. To trawl (the reference being to the net being dragged along the seabed, by sail, steam or diesel). 2. A **drogue sail** (q.v.).

Drag-net: a seine net worked close to the beach, being paid out from a rowing boat (which followed a semi-circular course) and then hauled in when the vessel had returned to shore.

Draw-bucket: a large bucket used to collect seawater from over the side of a moving vessel. This had to be done carefully and correctly, by filling the container opposite to the direction of travel, in order for the person holding its rope not to be pulled overboard.

Draw-net: a drag-net.

Dress: to treat nets and sails with preservative materials.

Dressing: creosote, used as a preservative in new drift-nets.

Driers: chemical siccatives which were added to linseed oil, when preserving longshore drift-nets.

Drift: to catch pelagic species (primarily herring, mackerel and sprats) with drift-nets.

Drifter: a fishing vessel (powered, successively, by sail, steam and diesel) which operated drift-nets and caught herrings and mackerel.

Drifter pictures: ship portraits of (mainly) steam drifters, which were produced for vessel-owners and crew members (especially skippers). See also, **Pierhead painters**.

Drifter-trawler: a steam or diesel vessel which operated both drifting gear and trawls, according to the season, and could thus keep working all year round. Steam drifters and drifter-trawlers of the "classic era" (c.1910-39) were usually around 75 to 85 feet long, by 18-20 feet in the beam, and drew 8-9 feet of water.

Drift-net: a long, rectangular net which (with others attached to it) floated on the tide, in the upper reaches of the sea, to catch pelagic species such as herrings, mackerel and sprats.

Drive: to drift along on the tide with a fleet of nets out.

Drive down: to drift with the ebb tide.

Drive off: to make headway, or speed, in a steam or diesel vessel.

Drive up: to drift with the flood tide.

Driver: the engineer on board a steam drifter. The name probably derives from the fact that, in the early days of steam propulsion in the herring fleets (late 1890s/early 1900s), most of the engineers were men from inland who had experience of "driving", or operating, steam threshing equipment and who filled in a period of traditional unemployment after harvest by becoming involved in the autumn **Home Fishing** (q.v.).

Drogue-sail: a triangular piece of canvas mounted on a steel frame, which was thrown over the stern of a smack, as it entered harbour, to fill with water and slow the vessel down. The word *drogue* may be a variant of *drag*.

Drop on: to encounter, or find, shoals of herring.

Drowned herring(s): dead fish that had been in the drift-net meshes for such a prolonged period that the gills had ceased to function.

Duck: a Fleetwood term for the Haddock (*Melanogrammus aeglefinus*), which is simply use of the second syllable of the word as a variant abbreviation.

Duck-light: a flat-bottomed oil-lamp with projecting wick.

Dudder: to shake, quiver, or vibrate. The expression usually refers to the vibration of trawl warps while towing was in progress, but was occasionally used to describe the shudder felt when a trawler came fast to its gear. The word can be traced back to the middle of the seventeenth century.

Duff-chokers: A Lowestoft nickname for fishermen from Great Yarmouth – a reference, no doubt, to the **light duff** (q.v.), which was a staple item of food on board ship, and a title that was given in retaliation for being called **pea bellies** (q.v.).

Duffel: thick woollen cloth, with a heavy nap, which took its title from a town of that name in Belgium, where the material was first made.

Dump: to jettison unsellable fish. The term was used particularly of herrings during the 1930s, when periods of glut led to the price at market falling away to nothing. At such times, the drifters either returned to sea and dumped their catches close to land or (more usually) landed the fish and left it on the quayside. Local farmers could then collect it for manure, or it might find its way to the herring reduction factory at Great Yarmouth, where it was converted into fish-oil.

Dump-heads/ends: the rounded ends of the quays on Lowestoft fish market, particularly those at the entrance to Waveney Dock.

Dust: a smacksman's term for **stocker bait** (q.v.) – presumably because the extra money (such as it was) was small in value and derived from the sale of species that were of no great significance on the market. Alternatively, the word might conceivably have been an ironic abbreviation of *gold-dust*, because any top-up on wages was welcome – however modest.

Dutch farts: Sea-urchins – especially the Green Sea-urchin (*Psammechinus miliaris*).

Dutchmen's mudballs: a politer term than the one immediately above. Sea-urchins, if trawled up in large numbers, were a considerable nuisance to the fisherman. The uncomplimentary Dutch reference was the result of centuries of maritime rivalry between England and Holland.

E

Earwigging: listening in on the fishing radio-band at sea, in order to gather news and information. Most valued of all were any references to good catches being made – especially when the locations were mentioned. Many skippers were close-lipped when it came to divulging such information, but there were occasions when information was shared – usually to relatives or to colleagues working for the same company.

East-and-west boats: cargo vessels plying between England and Holland, with processed fish (mainly processed herrings) being conveyed on the outward run and with butter carried on the return journey.

Elliott pot: a small, two-cylinder steam engine with an upright boiler and narrow funnel, made by the Beccles firm of Elliott & Garrood, generating something like 15-20 horsepower. A number of these engines were fitted into the first generation of steam drifters, before being superseded by bigger and more powerful units.

Eye: a loop made in the end of a rope.

F

Fair-lead: a device (sometimes movable, sometimes fixed) with a hole or holes in it, which allowed a rope to pass freely in either direction.

Fairway: a fair-lead.

Fall away: to drop, or decrease in strength (a term always used of the wind).

False bellies: old pieces of net, which were fitted to the underneath of a trawl's cod-end, to minimise wear and tear on that part of the gear.

Fang(s): propeller blade(s). The analogy here would seem to be the shape of teeth.

Fang a hold: to take hold; to grasp. "Fang a hold o' this" was a common command, at one time.

Fantails: squid – notably, the Northern Squid (*Loligo forbesi*), which was often taken in trawls. They were sometimes sold to **longliners** (q.v.) on return to port.

Farlane(s): large, deep wooden troughs into which herrings were put prior to being gutted for Scotch cure.

Fastener: 1. The act of a trawler fouling an underwater obstruction while fishing, thereby causing it to **come fast** (q.v.). 2. The obstruction itself.

Fear-nots: fishermen's heavy, woollen, white trousers. The term is a variant of *fearnought*, a late eighteenth century word for a thick woollen cloth, once used for seafarers' coats and porthole covers.

Fender: 1. A heavy length of wood used to break in new **manila** (q.v.) warps. It was tied to one end of the rope (the other being secured somewhere on board) and thrown overboard, to be towed along and act as a means of stretching the fibres. 2. A buffer of wood or rope (even a car tyre) hung over a boat's side to protect it from collisions with dock walls or other vessels.

Fetch: 1. To reach harbour or safe anchorage – a nautical term dating from the middle of the sixteenth century. 2. The distance required for wind and tide to travel to produce waves of a particular size.

Fid: a long, tapering, wooden or metal spike which was used to force the strands apart when **splicing** or **bending** (q.v.) ropes. The word is of unknown origin.

Fiddle-fish: the Monkfish (*Squatina squatina*), a member of the shark family. See Appendix 1, no. 22.

Fiddley: a grating above the engine-room on a drifter or drifter-trawler. It was a favourite place for crew members to sit in cold weather, because of the heat which rose from below. As one of the writer's respondents once recalled: "If you wanted a warm, you used t' park yuh stern on the fiddley."

Fifie: A Scottish two-masted sailing drifter with dipping **lugsails** (q.v.) fore and aft, which was associated originally with the county of Fife and the port of Anstruther in particular. The design was so good that the vessel (together with its successor, the Zulu) became the classic boat of Scotland in the pre-steam era. Large numbers came to East Anglia each year, to take part in the autumn herring voyage – a migration that had begun with boats from the Firth of Forth in the 1860s.

Figure-eight: the knot that secured the tie around a drift-net at the end of a voyage and indicated to net-store staff that the meshes were damaged. It was also commonly referred to as a **single knot** (q.v.).

Fill out: to unload herrings from a drifter.

Fill up/filling: the term used of herring recovering and fattening up after spawning.

Fine cure: lightly salted herrings.

Fine down: to become calm(er) – a term always used of weather conditions.

Fine nets: Scotch nets; i.e. drift-nets with cotton meshes, as opposed to the older coarser variety which were made from hemp twine.

Fire: a term used to describe the phosphorescence visible at night, near the surface of the sea, caused by shoals of herring, mackerel or sprats.

Fireman: 1. The **trimmer** (q.v.), on board a steam trawler. 2. The Great Yarmouth term for the **stoker** (q.v.), on board a steam drifter.

Firsts: top-quality smoked herrings (especially kippers).

Fish-bags: net bags into which fish were put (after being gutted) and towed along in the water beside a **smack** (q.v.) so as to clean them thoroughly and ensure that they would have a good appearance when laid out for sale on the market. Smacks' catches usually fetched a better price than those of steam trawlers because their method of fishing was gentler and less damaging, resulting in a better-quality product for both the retail and restaurant trades.

Fish-finder: a sonar device, used for locating shoals of herring and mackerel.

Fish-hold: the below decks storage-area in which catches were stowed away.

Fish-house: an alternative term for a **smokehouse** (q.v.) and one that was of greater age. It can be found in use in late medieval documentation.

Fish Labs (The): the research laboratory facility located at Pakefield Road, Lowestoft, on the site of the former *Grand Hotel*, and currently run by DEFRA (Dept. for the Environment & Rural Affairs) under the acronym CEFAS (Centre for Environment, Fisheries and Aquaculture Science). It moved to this premises in 1955 from a building further to the north, on the Southern Esplanade, and remains one of the most important marine research agencies in Europe. For many years, it was referred to alternatively as MAFF (Ministry of Agriculture, Fisheries & Food).

Fish-room: a name for the main fish-hold on a large trawler (especially the kind which worked distant waters), where the catches were often gutted as well as stored.

Fish tackle: a strop and hook used to hoist the **cod-end** (q.v.) of a trawl inboard (especially on a smack's beam trawl).

Fish-trawl: a term sometimes used by **longshoremen** (q.v.) to describe a beam-trawl used to catch demersal species (such as dabs and soles), as opposed to the one employed when shrimping. There was quite a difference in the mesh-size and rig of the respective nets, and sometimes in the length of the beams used – depending on the size of individual vessels. In Lowestoft and Pakefield, *fish-trawls* would have a length of eight to fifteen feet, whereas *shrimp-trawls* might go down to six feet or so. Boats from Great Yarmouth and Gorleston tended to use the bigger size of beam for both modes of fishing.

Fisher-girl: a Scottish female, of widely varying age ("Anything between fifteen and seventy," the writer was once told), who gutted and packed herrings for export and who followed the Scottish drifter fleet from port to port.

Fisherman's knot: a means of joining two cords or narrow diameter ropes. An overhand knot was tied in the end of one of the cords or ropes and the end of the other one pushed through it. An overhand knot was then tied in this, encircling the first cord or rope. When both free ends were pulled, the two knots slid towards each other, tightened and made a neat join.

Fishing chaps: a term that was used by people, living in inland villages, of men from the rural areas who went to sea – particularly the younger men. *Chap* is an abbreviated form of *chapman* (an itinerant hawker of some kind), which developed its general meaning of a male of some kind during the early eighteenth century.

Five-fingers: starfish of any kind, but particularly the Common Starfish (*Asterias rubens*).

Fixing: a contract made between **fisher-girls** (q.v.) and Scotch curers, in the winter months, setting out terms of employment for the former party during the coming summer and autumn herring seasons. Also see, **Arles**.

Flag: the signal used, during the 1930s period of controlled fishing at Great Yarmouth and Lowestoft, to inform steam drifters that they could put to sea.

Flake: a fishmonger's term, on the South Coast, for dogfish – either the Spur-dog (*Squalus acanthias*) or the Lesser-spotted Dogfish (*Scyliorhinus caniculus*).

Flakes: the serpentine folds of a rope, laid out to dry after preservative treatment. The operation of laying out a rope in this fashion is known as *flaking down*.

Scots **fisher-girls** at Great Yarmouth, in front of barrels of pickled herrings. When not **gipping** and packing herring, they would frequently be found knitting. They are knitting 'in the round' on several needles, probably making **ganseys**.

Flapper: a piece of net at the entrance to a trawl's cod-end, which allowed fish to go in but prevented their escape.

Flat-a-calm: a calm sea, with no movement of wind or water. Such conditions were sometimes referred to as a *dead calm*.

Flats: a Fleetwood term for plaice, dabs, witches, flounders etc.

Flea and Bug Row: an alternative version of **Bug and Flea Terrace** (q.v.).

Fleet: 1. A drifter's complement of nets. 2. A number of vessels (large or otherwise) trawling co-operatively and running catches to a **cutter** or **mother ship** (q.v). The word *fleet* itself derives from the Old English *flēot*, meaning "a ship", or "ships".

Fleeter: an individual vessel involved in co-operative trawling.

Fleeting: company practice, whereby substantial numbers of vessels trawled co-operatively with a master-skipper (sometimes referred to as an *admiral*) in overall charge to direct operations. This was found to be economically advantageous, but it was socially and psychologically bad for the fishermen, who were continuously at sea for weeks at a time. The "golden age" of fleeting, in the North Sea, was the last quarter of the nineteenth century – but conditions on board ship were so bad for the men that it was customary to talk of being "sentenced to the Dogger". The term later became applied to any kind of co-operative fishing where a number of vessels were involved, whether drifting or trawling.

Flit-boat: a converted Scottish sailing drifter, with diesel engine added and the fish-hold gutted out, which conveyed coal and other cargo around the Shetland Isles. The term obviously derives from the verb meaning "to move about from place to place".

Flitting: the trading conducted by, or with, a flit-boat.

Float: a lightship – the term reflecting the vessel's lack of an engine and simply riding to its anchor and chain.

Floating fish: demersal fish, of the cod group, which swim up above the seabed.

Flopper: a variant of **flapper** (q.v.).

Flow: the slack in a trawl-net's lower **wings** (q.v.), which was necessary for the gear to function effectively.

Flower o' dell: the Cuckoo ray (*Raja naevus*). The reference here is to the roundels on the fish's wings resembling flower-heads.

Fluke: 1. The triangular end on the arm of an anchor, which engages with the seabed. 2. The Flounder (*Platichthys flesus*), whose name has antecedents in the Old Swedish *flundra* and the Danish *flynder*.

Flutter: a word used to describe the disturbance caused on the surface of the sea by the shoaling activity of mackerel.

Flying squad: a gang of coopers and Scotch girls, whose task it was to finish off the pickling process by topping up and sealing the barrels of fish. The image created by the term is one of speed and high activity – with overtones of Scotland Yard's once-famed, specialist detective branch.

Foc'sle: a space in the bows of a vessel, which served as crew quarters. The word is an abbreviated form of the old term, *forecastle*, which harks back to the time (in the medieval period) when larger craft had a raised and battlemented deck at the front.

Foc'sle funnel: the flue which led from the foc'sle stove.

Following sea (a): the term used of when wind and tide combined to create large waves, which moved in the same direction as the course taken by a vessel. Such conditions were among the most dangerous at sea, especially for trawlers with their gear down.

Footings: the **perk boards** (q.v.) of a steam drifter.

For'ad: the front section, or area, of a vessel. The word is a simple abbreviation of *forward*.

Fore-deck: the forward, or front, deck of a craft.

Fore-hold: a fish-hold in the bow section of a drifter or trawler.

Forelock: the eye at the end of a drift-net's **heading** (q.v.) cord.

Fore-mast: the mast nearest to a vessel's bow.

Fore-peak: a small storage space in the bow of a vessel, used for spare ropes etc. The term may be compared with the Dutch *voorpiek*.

Fore-room: another name for the fore-hold. The word *room* was often used for below-deck spaces on fishing craft.

Fore-stay: the wire support, or guy, running from a vessel's foremast to the bow.

Fork(s): a Fleetwood term for small hake.

Forts: 1. Scotch-cure barrels only one-quarter full. 2. Haddock(s) between medium and large in size.

Forty Thieves: the name given in Lowestoft (mainly, during the 1930s) to the Hobson fish-selling company and its associates because of alleged sharp practice. The reference is plainly taken from the story of Ali Baba.

Frame: 1. The cords at the top, bottom and sides of a drift-net. 2. The skeleton of a fish. One of the writer's respondents once remarked, concerning skate that were taken by **longline** (q.v.) on grounds to the south of Ireland and which were in a highly emaciated state, "There wun't nothin' on 'em at all. All you had wuz the frame o' the fish."

Frap: a state of confusion, even of panic.

Frap/frap-up: a term used for drift-nets and warps getting tangled. There may be a link here with mid sixteenth century usage, when the word *frap* had the nautical meaning of "to bind tightly".

Freemason boats: Scottish drifters which carried the Freemasons' emblem of square and compasses on the bow or funnel. This denoted membership of the organisation on the part of the boat's owner. Freemasonry in Scotland was much more widespread among the working classes (for want of a better term) than it was in England and there were many more **skipper-owners** (q.v.) of Scottish vessels than was the case further south.

French gear: the Vigneron-Dahl refinement of the **otter trawl** (q.v.), introduced into Britain from France in 1922. Vessels belonging to the Cardiff firm of Neale & West were among the first to adopt it and a patent-royalty was payable to the French government for its use.

French-letter boots: rubber sea-boots. The "latex connotation" requires no comment!

Fresher: 1. A German freighter which conveyed **klondyke herrings** (q.v.) from Lowestoft to Altona. 2. A merchant who traded in fresh herrings for home business or for export.

Freshing port: a port which handled fresh herrings only. Some of the smaller Scottish fishing-stations fell into this category.

Fry: the term used for a sufficient quantity of fish (herrings or sprats) to provide a meal for a given number of people. The usual reference would have been to a family group or a boat's crew. Frying herrings, or sprats, in a pan was very much the traditional way of cooking them.

Frying trade: fish and chip shop enterprises.

Fulls: 1. An official Scottish Crown Brand category: herrings not less than 10¼ inches long, with milt and roe in them. 2. More loosely, any herrings that had milts or roes in them.

Funny: very. The use of this word is still common today in the Lowestoft area. "I wuz funny scared" or "That come over funny dark"; such utterances would be immediately understood.

Furlane(s): a variant pronunciation of **farlanes** (q.v.).

G

G-link: a split link on an otter door's bracket (not unlike a capital G in shape), into which the warp's clip-link fitted for the trawling operation to be carried out.

Gaff: see **Garf(t)** below for fishermen's usual pronunciation of the word, and for its meanings.

Gale o' wind: the usual term for a high wind at sea.

Galley: a ship's kitchen, where meals were prepared.

Gallus(es): the metal frame(s), like an inverted U in shape, from which was suspended a block over which the trawl warp ran. The **doors** (q.v.) of otter trawls hung secured from the galluses when not in use. The word *gallus* itself is a variant of "gallows".

Gang: an abbreviated form of *gangway*.

Gangway: 1. The opening in a vessel's **bulwarks** (q.v.), by which people boarded or left the ship. 2. A gap in the **rail** (q.v.) of a vessel, through which a rope ran. 3. A space in the bulwark of a smack, through which the little boat was launched if need arose.

Gansy, Gansey: a Guernsey; a fisherman's heavy-knit jumper or top (often made of oiled wool, to give water-proofing qualities). The Channel Islands were a traditional source of high-quality knitwear, but East Anglian pronunciation of the word here makes it hard to recognise at first sight. However, the alteration of the vowel sound is authentic. Consider what might be done even today in the Lowestoft/Great Yarmouth area with the *-ĕr* phonetic component of a word: "He rid his bike down the street an' tanned the corner."

Garden lint: drift-nets that were no more use for fishing because of age (and the wear and tear it brought) or serious damage. They were sold off cheaply and usually cut up for garden nets.

Garnets: gurnards. Again, the word is the result of the peculiarities of East Anglian pronunciation.

Garf(t): 1. A gaff, used for bringing in fish when **longlining** (q.v.) This usually involved getting the instrument's hook into one of the gill-openings and lifting the fish inboard. 2. The movable spar which extends the head of a sail.

Gat: a navigable passage-way through coastal sandbanks. Two of the most notable ones along the East Anglian coast, allowing access to harbour, are the St. Nicholas (Great Yarmouth) and the Stanford (Lowestoft). The word derives from the Old Norse *gat*, meaning "an opening".

Gate: the method for tallying catches of herring unloaded from drifters at Lowestoft fish market. For each basket landed, the shore-workers chalked a short vertical line on one of the posts supporting the roof, thus: |. After four baskets had come ashore, the tally looked like this: | | | |. Once the fifth basket had been landed, a diagonal cross-stroke running from top left to bottom right was added. This continued until the whole catch had been discharged. Thus, the final count was done in fives and the total **crannage** (q.v.) worked out (each basket held a quarter-cran). The five-line symbol got its name from its similarity to a five-bar gate (though notably short of the two horizontal timbers!).

Gayback: the Mackerel (*Scomber scombrus*). The name focused on the fish's dorsal stripes and derived from Middle English usage, whereby *gay* (cf. Old French *gai*) meant anything bright or eye-catching. The writer's maternal grandparents commonly referred to the coloured cartoon strips in comics (like the *Beano* and *Dandy*) as *gays*. The 1960s saw the word increasingly used to mean "homosexual".

Gay-bowl: a Yarmouth term for the **monkey** (q.v.), a red and white chequered buff that was placed five nets from the end of a fleet of drift-nets to indicate that hauling was coming to an end. The *gay* element had exactly the same derivation as that immediately above.

Get in: to find a station at sea and begin fishing for herring. The term applied particularly to the East Anglian autumn voyage – especially on the grounds in the Smith's Knoll area, off the coast of Norfolk, where activity reached a peak and the waters became very congested.

Get the bang: to be dismissed from a job; to get the sack.

Gibbers: large haddock (but a size down from **jumbos**). The initial letter was pronounced as a hard g.

Gig: a fast, clinker-built rowing boat used by the beach companies for salvage work. It was smaller than a **yawl** (q.v.).

Gill: the side of a drift-net.

Gillded: a term used of pelagic fish snagged in the meshes by their gills and not removed by **scudding** (q.v.).

Gilldings: herrings left in the meshes after scudding. These were removed when the nets were cleaned and crew members were allowed to have them.

Gilson: a wire strop which runs through a sheave on a trawler's foremast and is used to hoist the cod end inboard (pronounced *jilson*).

Ginger-pop water: seawater which had been discoloured by herring shoals. The effect was caused by a combination of air-bubbles and fish-oil and it indicated that fish were present.

Gip/gyp: 1. To remove the gill(s) and gut of a herring, with a knife. 2. The gill itself.

Gipping: the process recorded in the first meaning given immediately above.

Glut: A superfluity of herrings landed and therefore no market for them.

Go about: to change tack.

Go-ashores: a fisherman's best clothes, for wearing on land when he wasn't working.

Go bang: to cease trading; go bankrupt. The term was used especially of Scotch curers during the 1920s, when that particular branch of the herring trade was facing great difficulty (caused by diminishing catches, the economic difficulties in post-war Europe, and the cancellation by the Communist government in Russia of debts incurred during the final years of the Tsarist regime).

Go on relief: a term used of driftermen who were out of work and had to seek poor relief. They were given tickets (vouchers) for food and other necessities and had to do useful work of some kind in return. Because they were paid by a **share system** (q.v.), they did not subscribe to an unemployment stamp and were classed as self-employed, and this meant that they were not entitled to dole payments. See also, **Test work**.

Go through: to become bankrupt.

Go to the other end: to haul drift-nets, starting at the farthest end from the boat. This was sometimes done in difficult weather conditions.

Go to work: to begin hauling nets.

Gobstick: a wooden disgorger for disengaging hooks from fish caught on **longlines** (q.v.). The association with the mouth area is obvious, *gob* being an old Gaelic word for the mouth.

Golden herring(s): herrings that had been fairly lightly salted in vats (for a day or so) and then smoked for about fourteen days. They were produced especially for trade with Mediterranean countries.

Gorger: a large, white-enamelled metal jug, used for serving tea on board fishing vessels. The name may have originated from the fact that its contents were swallowed avidly, if not greedily!

Grairpes: grapnels. The word is a variant pronunciation of *graips*, an East Anglian dialect word for "grippers" of one kind or another.

Grandfather: a large (and therefore old) fish of one kind or another. The term was applied particularly to the Sole (*Solea solea*) – especially at Padstow, where big specimens were taken during the 1920s by the Lowestoft **drifter-trawlers** (q.v.) on relatively unexploited grounds in the local Cornish waters. These were very rough on the fingertips of the men who handled and packed them on the market.

Granny: a wrongly tied reef knot, with the upper cross-over incorrectly formed. Any strain on the rope will cause the knot to jam and become very difficult to loosen. The name was probably a sexist reference to the ineptitude of women (and older women in particular) when it comes maritime matters.

Gratings: raised duckboards, set beside the fish-hold.

Green cod: an alternative term for the Coalfish or Saithe (*Pollachius virens*), which results from a particular tinge of colour in its skin and is reflected in the second element of its Latin species-name.

Greenhand: someone with no previous experience, who had just begun to go fishing – a variant, really, of *greenhorn*.

Grimmies/Grims: fishermen from Grimsby.

Gripe: the clamp and lashing which secured the **little boat** (q.v.) on the after-deck of a fishing vessel. The word is obviously a variant of *grip*.

Grit (The): the area of houses and service-buildings at Lowestoft, which was otherwise known as **The Beach** (q.v.) and which had developed on land between the bottom of the cliff and the shoreline. It was largely inhabited by people connected with fishing and the term recorded here takes account of the coarse, sandy soil on which the houses stood.

Gross earnings: The total value of a fishing vessel's earnings over the length of a voyage, without the running expenses being deducted.

Ground(s): particular area(s) of the seabed which yielded viable catches of fish and which the fishing craft therefore concentrated on.

Ground fish: demersal fish; those which lived on, or near, the seabed.

Ground-rope: a thick, heavy rope of eight to nine inches diameter on the bottom of a beam trawl's or otter trawl's net.

Growler: the Grey Gurnard (*Eutrigla gurnardus*). The fish acquired this name because, in common with other members of its family, it produces dull, grunting sounds from vibrating its swim-bladder. French fishermen recognised this characteristic in giving it the name *grognard*.

Grub-locker: the storage-space, or cupboard, on board ship in which the provisions were kept. It was not unknown for some of the older **smack** (q.v.) skippers to sleep on top of this, in order to prevent crew members from helping themselves to rations. On board trawlers, the food bill for a **trip** (q.v.) was divided by the number of men on board to ascertain average cost – and this was then deducted from the wages of the skipper and the mate. This was why some skippers (not all, by any means) were keen to keep food bills down to a minimum. As one of the writer's respondents wryly observed, "An extra pot o' jam used to be a crime!"

Grub up: 1. To provision a fishing vessel. 2. A lightship crewman's term for purchasing his own food for a tour of duty.

Guard(ed): the term used for putting the **oddy** (q.v.) on to drift-nets.

Guardfish: the Garfish (*Belone belone*). The term is a simple corruption of the name. Garfish were sometimes caught in drift-nets and were highly thought of as food by some fishermen, though others found the green skeleton off-putting.

Guarding meshes: the oddy of a drift-net.

Gun: the maroon that was fired to summon lifeboat crew to a rescue mission.

Gun-smacks: the term used by people in Lowestoft for the **armed smacks** (q.v.) which operated from the port during the First World War. Such decoy vessels (along with other secretly armed, non-Naval craft) were officially classified as *Q-ships* – the Q being selected as a non-explicit symbol of this class of boat.

Gurnet: a gurnard (again, variant pronunciation is in evidence).

Gut: a narrow passage of deeper water between two flanking sandbanks (e.g. the *Botney Gut*, at the southern end of the Dogger Bank). The word is recorded as early as the 1530s and might well have been a variant of *cut*, used in the sense of a quick route across or through something. Alternatively, it could be a variant of **gat** (q.v.).

Gut-barrel: the wooden container into which the **gut-tubs** (q.v.) were periodically emptied when herrings were being **gipped** (q.v.) for Scotch cure.

Gut-train: the locomotive and railway wagons which conveyed the waste from a fish market to wherever it was processed into meal or fertiliser.

Gut-tub: a half-section of a small wooden cask, which was placed in the **farlanes** (q.v.) at regular intervals to catch the herring guts removed during **gipping** (q.v.).

Gutting-girls: the Scottish women who processed pickled herrings.
Gutting up: the term used on board trawlers for eviscerating the fish caught in each **haul** (q.v.), prior to sending them down into the hold for storage.
Guy: a general name for a rope, or line, used to secure or steady something.

H

Haddock rash: irritation of the hands caused, when gutting, by the fish's stomach contents, which included finely eroded seabed debris. Some fishermen took the precaution of washing their hands regularly in disinfected water (Izal was commonly used) to counter the effects of this, and of other discomforts.
Half-and-half bidding: a method of buying fish at auction, whereby the purchaser offered to take a stipulated quantity at a final price that had had half of the preceding increment deducted.
Half-and-half-quarter: a crew member of a steam **drifter** (q.v.) who was paid on the basis of a ⅝ share. This was the rate usually given to the **cast-off** (q.v.).
Half-quarter: an eighth part of one individual share in the profits of a herring voyage. The term *eighth* was never used.
Half-sider: a steam trawler, or drifter-trawler, which was rigged for fishing on the starboard side only by having the fore and after **galluses** (q.v.) fixed there, but not to port. The starboard (right) side of a vessel was usually the one from which fishing gear was operated, but there were occasions when weather or tidal conditions were conducive to the port (left) side being used.
Ham: an area of low-lying, marshy ground close to the shoreline. There is a *ham* in South Lowestoft, in the old parish of Kirkley. The origin of the word may be the Old English *hem*, meaning "enclosed land", since any marshy area would have easily discerned margins.
Handkerchief: a smacksman's term for the smallest size of **jib** (q.v.) used (i.e. the storm-jib).
Handline: a fishing-line with varying kinds of hook attachments able to be used, which was worked over the side of a **drifter** by crew members as the vessel lay to its nets. Common demersal species were caught in this way and sold for pocket-money when the boat reached port. Use of a handline is recorded in apprentice agreements of the sixteenth century, when

young boys first went to sea and began their fishing careers, with half of the money deriving from use of the gear being theirs to keep.

Handspike: a stout wooden rod, used to lift a beam trawl's warp onto the **platten** (q.v.).

Hang (on): to drift with the tide (referring to a vessel), attached to a **fleet** (q.v.) of nets.

Hank(s): length(s) of rope, or cord – sometimes loosely looped. The word derives from Old Norse *hanka*, meaning "to coil".

Hansom cab/cart: an **aft-sider** (q.v.). The shape of the wheelhouse was supposed to resemble the sitting compartment of the famous two-wheeled, horse-drawn *cabriolet*.

Hard(s): firm areas of beach within a harbour, onto which boats could be drawn up out of the water for maintenance and repair. There is an old-established one in Gorleston, called *Darby's Hard*, on the west side of Great Yarmouth harbour.

Hard-cure: herrings which had been **roused** (q.v.) for two or three days, then smoked for a period of four to six weeks. The term was usually applied to **red herrings** (q.v.).

Harry Tate's Navy: the affectionate nickname given to the Royal Naval Patrol Service during the Second World War. Harry Tate was the stage-name of Ronald Hutchinson, a popular music hall comedian of the Edwardian era and the 1920s and 30s. Two of his favourite catch-phrases were "How's your father?" and "I don't think!", and part of his act consisted of expressed confusion when dealing with modern technology of the time. It was this particular feature that became an ironic comment on the fishing vessels brought into service to monitor the movements of "high-tech" German fighting craft.

Harvest of the Seas: a maritime version of the harvest festival service, which was held in coastal communities towards the end of the autumn herring season to give thanks for the ocean's yield. The celebration was popular during the late Victorian period and up to the outbreak of World War II, but declined throughout the 1950s and 60s. It was customary to decorate churches and chapels with all kinds of artefacts associated with fishing: nets, buffs, baskets, wooden shovels, vessels' pennants and flags, and even strings of red herrings.

Harwich: this word is always pronounced *harridge* and it has two specific uses. One is to suggest a state of confusion and being unprepared (e.g. "She come knockin' at the door an' I wuz all of a Harwich."). The other is connected with devout people, who were careful with the language they used and would not therefore make any direct reference to Hell (e.g. "Well, I'll go t' Harwich!"). The former reference is said to derive from an occasion when George II, on a return journey from Hanover, suddenly turned up in Harwich and caught everyone unawares. This was probably in 1737, when His Majesty came ashore at Lowestoft, suffering very badly from sea-sickness. After a period of time allowed for his recovery, he continued his journey to London by coach, stopping at Harwich on the way.

Haul: to pull fishing-nets in, whether by hand or mechanical means.

Haul for mother: the last haul of a trip on board a trawler. The implication here is that some of the fish (being the freshest) would be taken home by crew members for their families. It was not unknown for some of the more unscrupulous Lowestoft trawler-skippers to shoot their gear on Sheringham Bank, off the North Norfolk coast, and drag up the local fishermen's crab and lobster pots. These were then emptied and thrown back into the sea, with their catches becoming the perquisite of the crew.

Haul King George's trawl: an ironic utterance (intended to be humorous) which was made on board the **armed smacks** (q.v.) of the First World War, when hauling began. The boats' owners received charter money from the Royal Navy for their craft, but got nothing from the sale of any fish caught. That money went into government funds.

Hawker: an itinerant fish-seller, who worked his way round inland villages. The word derives from either Low Dutch or Low German origins: *heuker* or *höker*.

Hawseman: a member of a steam drifter's crew, below the mate in rank. He was paid a full share and may originally (in the days of sail) have been in charge of the vessel's ropes. The initial h was often dropped by crew members, in enunciation of the term, making it sound like **oarsman** (q.v.). *Hawse* itself would appear to be an abbreviation of *hawser*.

Hawse-pipe: the hole in a vessel's bow through which the anchor chain, or cable, ran.

Head(ing) the sea: an expression used of a vessel with its bow meeting the flow of the tide, usually applied when it was stationary (or barely making way) while fishing gear was being cast or hauled.

Headfish: prime fish. The meaning of *head*, in this case, is "valuable," "important".

Head-line: 1. The cork-line on a **drift-net** (q.v.). 2. The upper rope on a trawl – either fixed to the beam (on a beam trawl) or carrying floats on an **otter trawl** (q.v.).

Head-rope: the cork-line on a drift-net.

Heading(s): the cords on the sides of a drift-net, which served to strengthen the net and give it shape.

Heave to: to bring a vessel to a halt, without anchoring.

Heave out: to cran out; unload herrings.

Heaving-line: a rope or cable on which a smack was **warped round** (q.v.) and out of dock, using its own steam capstan.

Heavy cure: well-salted herrings. The term usually applied to **rough packs** (q.v.).

Heel over: the term used of a sailing craft leaning to one side, as it made its way through the water. See also, **On the cant**.

Heft: a catch, or snag, which caused a rope to foul. The word may derive from *heave*, with its sense of weightiness and physical effort.

Helston Floral: the term used for the Helston *Furry Dance*, held annually on 8 May (an old medieval feast day known as The Apparition of St. Michael the Archangel). This celebration of Spring's arrival was as famous in its way as Padstow **May Day** (q.v.) and sometimes, if the Newlyn mackerel fishing season had gone on a little longer than usual, some Lowestoft fishermen made the effort to attend the event – before proceeding to Padstow to re-gear and catch soles.

Herring-slaughterer: a fisherman who worked on steam drifters.

Herring spink: the Goldcrest (*Regulus regulus*). It was given this nickname because migrants from Scandanavia sometimes alighted on drifters at sea during the autumn herring season. *Spink* was actually a Middle English word for a finch – especially the Chaffinch (*Fringilla coelebs*), whose two-note call is probably reflected in the name – and it remained in common use in East Anglia well into the second half of the twentieth century.

Hickety: moderately rough (a term always used of the sea). The term would seem to derive from *hick*, an East Anglian dialect word meaning "to hop", or one which implied irregular movement of some sort. For example: "He wun't half hickin' along on them crutches." Thus, the choppy movement of waves lends itself to description of this nature.

Hid-stifler: someone in charge of other people. Therefore, for *hid* read "head"! There is considerable irony in this expression, directed at those who give orders to lesser mortals.

Hides: cowhides which were fitted to the underside of a trawl's **cod-end** (q.v.) to reduce wear on that part of the gear. It tended to be vessels from Hull, Grimsby and Fleetwood which used them on distant-water voyages, and there are recorded instances of anthrax outbreaks among fishermen resulting from the use of infected, imported hides from Argentina. See also, **False bellies**.

Hipprodome: the herring sale-ring on Lowestoft fish market. This building was not only circular in shape, but full of activity and incident!

Hob mittens: fishermen's mittens made from white, oiled wool.

Hoddy: the oddy on a **drift-net** (q.v.). The retention and use of the *h* reflects the spelling commonly found in sixteenth and seventeenth century probate inventories.

Hold: a large, under-deck storage space found on fishing or merchant craft.

Holding marks: manilla strands that were secured to an otter trawl's warps in order to inform the mate when to brake the winch, as the warps were brought to the towing-block during hauling.

Hollabut: the Halibut (*Hippoglossus hippoglossus*).

Holy-rollers: Nonconformist Christians who belonged to no official denomination and who held religious services in their homes.

Home Fishing: the East Anglian autumn herring voyage. The vowel sound in *Home* was always pronounced in the same way as the double-o in words like "hook" and "took".

Honeysuckle twists: a polychaete marine worm of the Terebellidae family (specifically, *Amphitrite gracilis*), whose abdomen had a curl in it. The thorax and head of this creature were thought to resemble a honeysuckle flower and stamens.

Hoodway: the approach to the cabin or **foc'sle** (q.v.), which sometimes had protective sides and an overhang to keep out the weather.

Hook: an anchor of one kind or another.

Hook in: to gaff fish, which had been caught by **longlines** (q.v.), and to lift them inboard.

Hook on: to impale the bait (squid, whelks etc.) on longline hooks.

Horse: an iron guide on the foredeck of a **smack** (q.v.), along which the foresail sheet travelled. The image of a working animal is found transferred here to a mechanism performing a particular function.

Horse mackerel: the Scad (*Trachurus trachurus*). This pelagic species was greatly disliked by fishermen for a number of reasons: it had little or no commercial value; it was difficult to remove from the meshes of drift nets; and the spines on its first dorsal fin could cause a painful puncture to the hands. If any quantity of scads were taken (particularly on the Westward voyage), they were usually given away or sold cheaply to French **longliners** (q.v.).

Horse-marines: horse mackerel, as immediately above. The word *horse*, in this case, means something coarse or rough in quality (e.g. horse mushrooms, horseradish).

Hospital ground: a term used for areas of the seabed, where various species of demersal fish were found with sores and abrasions on their bodies. It was the belief of some fishermen that the fish had congregated there to be healed by some property or other in the environment. One particular part of the **Dogger Bank** (q.v.) was actually officially known as *The Hospital Ground* and recorded as such on charts. Fishermen noted cod, haddock, plaice and dabs all as having skin defects of one kind or another.

Hospital ship: a specialist vessel (often a converted trawler), with medical equipment and trained staff on board, which accompanied the fishing fleets of some European nations while they were working **distant water** (q.v.) grounds. It was a practice not adopted in Britain, but one which was admired by its fishermen.

Hoss-pissy water: seawater stained brown by the phytoplankton *Phyœcystis* – a less polite term than the **baccy juice** cited earlier.

Hoss-pittle: the same reference as immediately above.

Hot-bulb engine: an early type of internal combustion engine fuelled by paraffin.

Hound: either the Lesser-spotted Dogfish/Rough Hound (*Scyliorhinus caniculus*) or the Larger-spotted Dogfish/Nurse Hound (*Scyliorhinus stellaris*).

House-flag: a fishing company's badge or emblem painted on the funnels of its vessels, or that of individual boat-owners given the same treatment.

Hovel: a salvage claim made against the owners or insurers of any vessel rescued at sea and towed into port. The term may originate from the fact that the **beachmen** (q.v.), who specialised in the business of salvage and wreck, originally operated from sheds and lean-tos on the shoreline.

Hoveller: a sturdy, broad-beamed beach boat used in salvage work and **longshore** (q.v.) fishing.

Hubbard's Rocks: an area of brick rubble and other debris off Pakefield beach, created by the destruction of houses at the hands of the sea during a period of serious erosion lasting from 1900-1907. Throughout the 1920s and 30s, this artificial reef led to good catches of crab and cod – but after the Second World War it became less productive because of its gradual dispersal and sanding-over. The exact identity of the man who gave his name to the feature has never been established.

Hubble: a corruption of hovel, as above.

Hughie and Rolph: an onomatopoeiac term for seasickness (e.g. "I wuz Hughie an' Rolf for the first three or four days, that trip"). In order for the image to work, one has to speak this phrase aloud, with as much guttural emphasis as possible on the two names.

Hunch: a hunk of (usually) bread.

Husky: A South Coast term for the Larger-spotted Dogfish/Nurse Hound. The dog connection here is obvious, but it is also worth mentioning that the word *huss* is an old dialect term for dogfish generally, regardless of specific type. It is interesting that the first recorded medieval usage is rendered as *huske*.

Huts (The): two-storey, terraced wooden buildings (eight rooms up, eight down, was a common size) located on the waterfront in Lerwick harbour – often with a balcony on the upper floor – which provided accommodation for **Scotch girls** (q.v.) during the summer herring season. They were a distinctive feature of the local townscape and were fondly remembered (and their occupants also) by many Lowestoft and Yarmouth driftermen, for the friendly social interchange which took place in the port.

I

Ice-box: a tin or zinc-lined compartment in a smack's fish-hold, used to store ice.

Ice down: to sprinkle crushed ice onto the layers of gutted fish, stored in the **pounds** (q.v.) of a trawler's hold.

Ice factory: established in Lowestoft (in 1898) to produce ice artificially, because of growing demand for the product by an expanding fishing industry and also because of the increasing price of natural ice. This was cut from the Norfolk Broads and from the local broad at Oulton, when these stretches of water were suitably frozen during the winter months, and it was also shipped in from the Norwegian fjords. The facility stood at the bottom of Riverside Road, on the south side of the inner harbour, next to the Maconochie (later Co-op) canning factory and was in operation until replaced in 1962 by a new works situated on the Fish Market itself, alongside Battery Green Road. The ice was produced in large blocks, which were then crushed up for use at sea or on land – whatever was required.

Icing back: a term used on fish markets for the re-icing of trawlfish which had been left unsold at the weekend and which had then to be kept in reasonable condition for the resumption of trading on Monday morning.

Improver: a young **beatster/beetster** (q.v.), who had completed the first year of her apprenticeship and who was then fully qualified at the end of the second.

Inside: close to land.

Inside fishing: fishing that was conducted close to the shore.

Inspector: an employee of a company purchasing **pickled** (q.v.) herrings, who scrutinised the contents of a certain number of barrels (chosen at random) to ensure that the quality of the product was up to the required standard.

Iron-bound: a term relating to trawls used for distant-water fishing in the Arctic, on which the **ground-rope** (q.v.) had spherical steel bobbins affixed along the whole of its length, from door to door.

Iron decks: the decks of First World War **standard trawlers** (q.v.), which were made from steel plates not wooden planking. It was the opinion of men who worked on them, during the 1920s and 30s, that these vessels were particularly noisy because of the way that impact-sound (even that made by people walking up and down) was transmitted to the spaces below decks.

Items and dittoes: a picturesque description of a fisherman's small effects taken on board and kept in his **ditty-box** (q.v.).

Ivy-leaves: small plaice (the analogy here is one of shape, of course).

Ixnay-oxnay: a term the writer once heard used to describe the **double-talk** (q.v.) employed by members of the Lowestoft **beach companies** (q.v.) to obscure the meaning of what they were saying when people outside their coterie were present.

J

Jacky: a small triangular topsail, which was used on smacks and sailing drifters during the autumn and winter months, when less sail area was usually required. The term probably derives from traditional use of the word *jack* to mean "something small".

Jam up: to steam against the tide. The image is one of a vessel working hard against the current, with restricted headway being made.

Jellied: a term used of drift-nets which had had jellyfish caught in them, while fishing was in progress. The effects of this were felt by the net-store workers when they came to service the gear at the end of a voyage. They suffered irritation and discomfort to hands and face from the dried deposits left in the meshes' fibres. One of the worst places for jellyfish infestation was the fishing grounds off North Shields, worked during the summer herring season. Various kinds of protective headgear were improvised by some of the fishermen to reduce the discomfort of getting stung, including old sou'westers worn back-to-front with eye-holes cut in. The writer was even told of one case where a metal bucket was used – again, with eye-holes present.

Jellies: jellyfish, of any kind. The types most commonly encountered were the Common Jellyfish (*Aurelia aurita*), the Compass Jellyfish (*Chrysaora hysoscella*), *Cyanea lamarckii*, *Cyanea capillata* and *Rhizostoma pulmo*.

Jennie brand: canned herrings produced in the Co-op processing factory at Lowestoft during the 1920s and 30s (premises which had previously belonged to Maconochie Bros). The label on the tins showed a typical **Scotch girl** (q.v.), in oily skirt, carrying two creels of herring. The name *Jennie* was chosen because it was seen as being typically Scottish, even to the point of being used as a generic nickname at one time for a woman from north of the border.

Jenny: 1. The abbreviated slang term for an electrical generator on board ship. 2. The fish referred to immediately below.

Jenny/jinny ray: the Starry Ray (*Raja radiata*), a popular variety with fish and chip shop proprietors to provide small "skate wings" for frying.

The word *jenny* itself possibly refers to the fish being one of the smaller members of the ray family, deriving from traditional use of the word to describe female animals (e.g. *jenny-ass*) – which are often smaller than the males.

Jew-boy trade: the export to European countries and to the USA of *roll-mop* herrings, produced in Lowestoft during the 1920s and 30s by the North Shields company, F.H. Phillips. The term reflects the popularity of this sweet-cure product among people of the Jewish faith, from whom it had probably originated in the first place.

Jew-killers: a nickname given to Gorleston beachmen (and which was soon applied to the population at large) during the first half of the nineteenth century. There are two versions of the story. The first is that, while engaged on a salvage and rescue mission, certain beachmen cut the finger from a stricken passenger of the Jewish faith (in order to get his ring) and left him to drown. The second says that Gorleston people were so close-knit and tight-fisted that even a Jewish man of business could not make a living in the town. There is no evidence that either story is true. The likelihood is that both of them were fabricated in Great Yarmouth, to the detriment of its smaller neighbour.

Jib: a triangular sail (of varying size according to wind-strength), set on a stay running from the top of the foremast to the outer end of the bowsprit. It was an important and steadying influence in the handling qualities of a **smack** (q.v.).

Jigger: 1. A large, rectangular topsail, which was commonly used on sailing drifters during periods of fine weather. 2. A lure used for mackerel, which consisted of a cylindrical lead weight with five or six hooks attached, onto which feathers (or even pieces of silver paper) were fixed. When this was drawn through the water on the end of a line, the movement of the feathers (or the silver paper) simulated the swimming of immature herrings or sprats, and the mackerel took the bait.

Jinny henniven: the *Jenny ray*, as referred to above.

Jive: the term used of a smack (and of other sailing craft as well) running before the wind, with mainsail and boom swinging from side to side. The word is obviously a variant, a mispronunciation even, of *gybe* – a late seventeenth century term, which itself derived from the Dutch *gijben*.

John o' Dora: the John Dory (*Zeus faber*). This species was sometimes referred to as *St. Peter's Fish*, because the apostle is said to have once drawn a gold coin from its mouth. The dark blotches, one on either side of its body, supposedly represent his finger and thumb marks. There are also other versions of the story, connected with the "miraculous draught of fishes" (John 21. 1-13), for which see **Peter's fish**. The name *John Dory* itself probably derives from the Latin word *janitor* ("the doorkeeper").

Jonah: 1. A boat which earned very little money. 2. A crew member, or outside person even, who was reckoned to bring bad luck to a vessel. The reference comes directly from the Old Testament (Jonah 1. 1-17), in the story of the man whom God required to go and preach against the city of Nineveh, but who decided that such a mission was not for him and took ship for Tarshish. During a great storm at sea, which was sent by God as retribution, Jonah had the courage to declare that he was the cause of the ship's distress and told the crew to throw him overboard in order to save their vessel and themselves. This having been done, Jonah was swallowed by a sea monster (traditionally said to have been a whale), but survived the ordeal and lived to carry out the task of ministry required of him.

Joskin: a countryman/farmworker, who went herring fishing in the autumn after the harvest was in and the autumn ploughing and sowing finished. A period of unemployment or casual work then followed, so to join a drifter in either Great Yarmouth or Lowestoft was a means of continuing to earn. The availability of this pool of labour in the hinterland of the two ports referred to was a major factor in the expansion of the fishing industry (especially herring-catching) during the second half of the nineteenth century, when the men's muscle-power was used to turn the hand-capstans when pulling in the nets (the practice is referred to in the folksong *Gorleston Light*, in the refrain "Haul, you joskins, haul" – see Appendix 2). Later on, when steam-capstans were introduced, the countrymen continued to go to sea. The word *joskin* itself is a late eighteenth century term for a country bumpkin and Charles Lamb used it in one of his essays.

Ju-ju: the Skate (*Raja batis*). The term is a variant of *jujube*, because gelatine made from skate-bones was used in making certain kinds of sweet during the 1920s and 30s. It is possible that the North Sea fishing song, *Sailing over the Dogger Bank*, makes a passing reference to the term in part of its chorus: "Watch her, stop her; we're proper juba-ju..." (see Appendix 2). On the other hand, the term may be a variant of *jubilee*.

Jumbo: any large type of demersal fish – the name deriving from the famous elephant kept in the London Zoological Gardens during the earlier part of the nineteenth century.

Jumper: a hip-length calico **slop** (q.v.), worn by fishermen as a working garment. At one time (during the second half of the nineteenth century, particularly), Yarmouth fishermen tended to wear blue ones and Lowestoft fishermen tan or brown – the latter having been coloured by the same agent as the one used to preserve sails. See **Bark** (q.v.) or **Tan** (q.v.).

Junks: fish cutlets. The term is a variant or mispronunciation of *chunks*.

K

Kedge anchor: a small anchor which was run out from a vessel and dropped, so as to allow the vessel to move itself by winding in the cable attached. This was usually done to reach a desired mooring station. The word *kedge* itself probably derives from the Middle English *cagge*, meaning "to fasten" or "to tie".

Keel: a thick, black or blue pencil/crayon, used for marking barrels of pickled herring. The derivation here is interesting, for it would appear to hark back to a specific late medieval usage, whereby *keel* meant *reddle* or *ruddle*, or to mark something with this particular substance. Thus, a notable colour change is in evidence here – from red to black or blue. There was no such transformation in Thomas Hardy's character, Diggory Venn, in *The Return of the Native*. He dug reddle on Egdon Heath and bore the colour of his trade.

Kell/kill: an alternative name for a **smokehouse** (q.v.), or a compartment within the same. The word is a variant of *kiln*.

Kelly's eye: a linking ring on a Vigneron Dahl otter trawl's back-strop, connecting the door with the bridle when towing was in progress. The term derives from an old music hall reference to the one-eyed Australian outlaw, Ned Kelly, and it was also popularly used as part of the Bingo call for number one.

Kid: the deck area of a steam drifter between the hold **coamings** (q.v.) and the gunwale.

Kid-board: a wide wooden board placed diagonally between the edge of the coaming and the gunwale on a steam drifter, to allow easy passage inboard for mackerel nets when hauling began.

Kilder: a shallow wooden tub, used for oiling mackerel nets. The word may have been a derivative of *kilderkin*, a barrel of eighteen gallons capacity.

King Herring: 1. The Allis Shad (*Alosa alosa*). This fish was occasionally found in drift-nets and, because of its similarity to the herring and its larger size, was regarded as the "King Herring" or shoal-leader. Shads were always thrown back into the water, in the belief that they would lead future shoals into the waiting nets. 2. The title given to the herring generally in acknowledgement of its importance in the local maritime economy – a fact which is referenced in two local folksongs, *Haisboro' Light* and *Windy Old Weather* (see Appendix 2).

Kipper: a herring that is gutted, split along the backbone, soaked in brine for half an hour or so, then smoked overnight. This particular type of cure was first practised in Scotland, using salmon, and was applied to herrings by John Woodger of Newcastle, in 1843, when he produced the first kippers at Seahouses, on the Northumbrian coast.

Kist: the wooden chest taken by **Scotch girls** (q.v.) on their travels around the British coasts, processing herrings, which contained their personal possessions, clothes etc. The word itself is an earlier form of *chest* and derives from Old Norse *kista*. It can be found in Middle English as *ciste*.

Kit: 1. Ten stones of trawlfish, by weight. 2. The wooden or metal tub which contained this quantity of fish. 3. A wooden tub or cask, of half-cran capacity, for handling **rough-pack** (q.v.) herrings. The term derives directly from the Middle Dutch word *kitte*, meaning "a tankard", and gives reference to the basic shape of the container in question.

Kites: wooden paravanes, used to keep an otter trawl's head-line floated up.

Kitten: a small catfish (i.e. Wolf Fish – *Anarhichas lupus*).

Klondyke: 1. The trade in salted and iced herrings to Altona, in Germany. 2. A nickname for the village of Kessingland in the early part of the twentieth century, prior to the outbreak of the First World War. This was because of the wealth reputedly present at the absolute height of the herring trade, owing to the fact that many of the leading Lowestoft steam-drifter owners lived there.

Klondyke boxes: wooden cases containing 12¼ stones of herring, for export to Germany – chiefly, for different kinds of processing and cure.

Klondyke herring: fish that were salted down directly in wooden cases, with a layer of ice spread over the top prior to the lid being nailed down, then transhipped to Altona (the out-port to Hamburg) for re-processing. This trade was started by a Lowestoft fish merchant, Benjamin S. Bradbeer, and it developed rapidly during the 1890s – thereby roughly coinciding with the Yukon gold-rush. Both were great wealth-producers, hence the name. *Klondyking* remained important to the Lowestoft economy right up to the Second World War.

Kneel: to heel over – a term used to describe a vessel leaning over or lying on its side. The word *heel* derives from the Old English *heald(an)*, meaning "inclined".

Knobbing: decapitating and gutting herrings in one process (done by a machine), prior to canning them. The term derives from *knob*, an eighteenth century slang term for the head.

Knock out: 1. Used as a verb, meaning to release the warps of an otter trawl from the **towing-block** (q.v.). 2. Used as a noun, meaning the calling-out of trawler crewmen to haul the net, leaving the chief engineer turned in.

Knoll (The): Smith's Knoll – a ridge in the seabed, thirty miles north-east of Lowestoft, which was the world's premier herring ground.

L

Laid up: the term used for a vessel which was moored or anchored somewhere, when not in use.

Landing: 1. The act of unloading fish at the market. 2. A term sometimes used of the quayside itself, especially if the outer wall was stepped to provide a lower working-surface. See **Lower landing**.

Landings: the cumulative quantity of fish on a market, following the vessels' unloading of catches.

Lane/lain: to tie **rough** (q.v.) mackerel nets together down their sides.

La(i)ning: the twine used to secure rough mackerel-nets in the manner described immediately above. *Laining* derives from the Old French *lanière*, meaning "a lace" or "a thong" (compare with *lanyard*).

Larnch: 1. To launch a boat (especially directly from the beach). 2. The instruction given on board a steam drifter to stop the capstan while nets were being hauled. The writer has never found, or been given, a plausible reason for this particular usage.

Last: an ancient measure that went well back into the medieval period and which, in the case of fishing, referred to one hundred **long hundreds** (q.v.) of herring or mackerel. At a count of roughly one thousand fish per barrel, this would produce twelve barrels. When used as a measure of weight for dry goods, the last was reckoned at two tons. The word derives from the Old English *hlæst*, meaning "a load" or "a burden".

Latchet: the Tub Gurnard (*Trigla lucerna*). The flesh of this fish was highly esteemed by smacksmen on account of its texture and flavour. A favourite way of cooking it was to bake it in an oven with meat-gravy and onions – treatment also given by Lowestoft fishermen to hake.

Lay in: to stay in harbour (usually because of bad weather).

Lay off: 1. To anchor offshore. 2. To mark out the lines of a vessel's hull (in French chalk) on the floor of the **mould-loft** (q.v.) in a shipyard, prior to the commencement of building. This would be done to full scale.

Lay up: 1. To tie up a vessel to a permanent mooring, when it was not in use for fishing. 2. To keep a boat head to wind. The expression was used particularly of strong southerly winds, in the North Sea, when the craft would be facing south. This was the direction in which the flood tide ran and was therefore "up" in fishermen's parlance.

Laylin twine: the heading cords on a rough mackerel-net. The word may well be connected with, or be a derivative of, **lane/lain** and **la(i)ning**, as outlined above.

Lazy deckie: a strop which was shackled to the fish tackle and used to pull up the cod-end during hauling. It worked off the trawler's winch and saved a great deal of human effort, hence the name.

Leach: the after-edge of a sail.

Leach-line: the **quarter-rope** (q.v.) on trawls (there were two of them), used to hoist the ground-rope inboard.

Lead(-line): a device used to measure the depth of water and assess the quality or type of seabed. It consisted of a long, cylindrical lead weight fastened to a length of rope, or cord. The other end of the weight was hollowed out. Fat or tallow (or even soap, on some occasions) was pressed into the hollow, which would cause particles from the seabed to adhere when the weight reached the bottom. This would enable fishermen to tell what kind of ground they were on. The depth calculation was made possible by the line itself having ties attached to it at one-fathom (six feet) intervals. It was customary to refer to it simply as *the lead*, as demonstrated in one of the verses of the folksong known as *Windy Old Weather* (see Appendix 2).

Leeboards: sturdy wooden panels, made of oak planks, which were carried on either side of some sailing vessels and let down into the water, as need arose, to check leeward drift. *Thames sailing barges* carried them; so did some of the heavily built Dutch **luggers** (q.v.).

Lee shore: a shore on to which the wind is blowing. In the days of sail it was hazardous for a vessel to be on a lee shore, as it would be in danger of being blown aground. The word *lee* would seem to derive from either the Old English *hlēo* or the Old Norse *hlē*.

Lee tide: a tide running in the same direction as the wind.

Leeward: the term used of a vessel moving away from the wind (especially when that movement was lateral or sideways). It was usually pronounced "lew'ard".

Legs: 1. The plaited **stopper** (q.v.), which held the warp to the towing-post on board a smack. 2. The short wire strops (two on each side of the trawl) which connected the otter doors to the net itself.

Lemon(s): the Lemon Sole (*Microstomus kitt*). This fish was highly rated by trawlermen for its texture and flavour.

Lemon dab: an alternative term for the Lemon Sole.

Lengthening-piece: a section of net, which was inserted into a trawl between the **cod-end** (q.v.) and the **belly/batings** (q.v.) in order to enable the gear to hold larger quantities of fish.

Let go: to cast off.

Life-jersey: the old-style cork lifejacket, worn by crews of the **sailing-and-pulling** (q.v.) lifeboats.

Light: often used as an abbreviation for *lighthouse* – as, for example, in the folksongs *Gorleston Light* and *Haisboro' Light* (see Appendix 2).

Light duff: dumplings made of self-raising flour and water and cooked by boiling gently for no more than half an hour. In inland, rural communities they were sometimes known as *twenty-minute swimmers* or *Norfolk dumplings*, and they were an important item of diet on the steam drifters especially. The recipe could vary slightly, according to individual taste and whim, and the word *duff* is a variant of *dough*.

Lighthouse: a vertical, steam **line-hauler** (q.v.), made by Elliott & Garrood of Beccles, which had a passing resemblance to the navigational aid.

Limit-line: the twelve-mile, territorial waters, exclusion zone agreed at the International Fisheries Convention of May 1882. By this agreement, all those European nations with a coastline bordering on the North Sea had exclusive right of fishery for their own native industry within a twelve-mile distance from shore. The term also applied to any variations of this agreement and any local bye-laws in Great Britain and Ireland which prohibited fishing of one kind or another in certain stipulated areas.

Line-hauler: a small winch, fixed to the side of a vessel, which facilitated the hauling of longlines. They were driven by steam power to start with, but were later succeeded by hydraulic and electrical models.

Liners: vessels which laid **longlines** (q.v.) and which were sometimes built specifically for this task.

Lining: fishing for demersal species by laying a series of baited lines (which were joined together in one continuous length) and weighting them down with anchors to the seabed.

Linseed oil: an extract from flax seeds, which was used to keep fishermen's oilskins and leather seaboots in good condition and which also served as a preserving agent for mackerel nets.

Lint: the meshes of a drift-net. The word refers back to the time (during the late medieval and pre-industrial eras) when some nets were made from flax fibre and others from hemp. *Lint* was an old name for flax, either as a plant or as fibre ready for spinning. Long after cotton had become the material used for drift-nets, the older term continued to be used – and it even carried on when, eventually, plastic monofilament superseded cotton.

Lint foot-rope: a technique employed on **longshore** (q.v.) drift-nets, whereby the bottom four to ten rows of meshes were rolled up and laced, thereby creating a means of weighting the nets down in the water.

Lipstick plaice: plaice that had become chafed around the mouth by digging themselves into the seabed during easterly winds (presumably to escape the effects of the swell caused). This was particularly noticeable in the North Sea during the winter months. The Plaice (*Pleuronectes platessa*) was, for much of the twentieth century, the staple trawl-fish species landed on the Lowestoft market.

Little Bethel: an alternative term for the **Beach Bethel** (q.v.), suggestive of its physical size when compared with the main non-denominational chapel opposite Lowestoft fish market.

Little boat: a drifter's or trawler's lifeboat – always mounted on the after-deck on steam or diesel vessels, but placed amidships on a smack.

Little boots: short, leather boots worn by fishermen, about mid-calf in length.

Liver-jar: small wooden casks used for storing cod livers on board trawlers. The livers were then processed into oil, on the return to port.

Liver-money: money paid to the crewmen on **distant-water** (q.v.) trawlers, which had derived from the sale of cod livers.

Lloyd George stamp: a generalised name for the National Insurance contributions introduced by David Lloyd George in 1912, which entitled those who paid to draw weekly unemployment benefit when they were out of work. Fishermen were not included in this scheme to begin with, but became eligible in 1921 when provision was extended – though not to drifter crew-members. The name of the originator was remembered in the term given here.

Log book: a record kept by some skippers of their fishing activity, year on year, noting quantities of fish caught in particular locations, at particular times of the year, and relating the catches to conditions of weather and tide. Any details written down were usually a closely guarded secret on the part of the men concerned and some of them even devised their own means of encoding the information. The story is told of one skipper who had encrypted his secrets and stuck them up, on the wheelhouse ceiling, on pieces of paper. "He had all these here hieroglyphics plastered up!" was the way that the writer had it described to him by one of his respondents.

Logie/logy: low in the water. The term was often used of the buffs on herring nets. If these were *logie*, it was usually the sign of a good catch of fish. The word is probably a corruption, or variant, of "low" rather than a derivative of the term which follows immediately below.

Logie/logy swell: a heavy ground-swell on the sea. The origin of the term would seem to be an American word of the mid nineteenth century, *logy*, which meant "heavy" in motion or in thought. This, in turn, probably derived from the Dutch *log*, meaning "heavy" or "dull".

Long boots: a fisherman's thigh-length seaboots – always made of leather, before this material eventually gave way to rubber.

Long fish: a term that was usually applied to ling and conger eel because of their distinctive shape, but was occasionally used with reference to cod and hake also.

Long hundred: 120 mackerel; 132 herrings. This term can be traced back well into the late medieval period when both these types of fish were counted out by hand, on being landed, in units of four (two in each hand). At some point, probably during the first half of the nineteenth century, the long hundred for herrings grew from 120 to 132 – undoubtedly the result of the buyers and merchants taking an opportunity to drive a harder bargain with the fishermen. See also, **Warp** (second definition).

Long-jawed: the expression used for a rope that had been over-stretched and had the turn taken out. Once this had happened, it was of little use – except for being unpicked and used for caulking planks.

Longline: a varying length of twine or cord, of different thickness and strength according to particular requirements, onto which hooks were affixed at periodic intervals (again, this varied). These hooks were baited with whatever was deemed to be suitable (whelk, squid etc.) and the line paid overboard, to rest upon the seabed and catch demersal species.

Longliner: a vessel which carried out the method of fishing described immediately above.

Longliner-man's knot: an alternative name for the **Fisherman's knot** (q.v.). It acquired the title here by being commonly used to join lengths of longline together.

Longshore: literally, "along the shore" – the term used of fishing activity carried out by small craft relatively close to land.

Longshore boat: a small craft propelled by oars and/or sail which often worked directly off the beach, fishing for various species according to the particular time of year.

Longshore herring(s): inshore herrings, caught by the type of boat described immediately above. The autumn ones were highly rated for their succulent eating qualities.

Longshoreman: a fisherman who made his living from working a longshore boat.

Longshores: longshore herrings.

Longshoring: to carry out small-scale fishing activity close to the shore.

Long-sleever: an elongated cloth bag or poke (sometimes made of canvas), with a draw-string, which was carried in the pocket and served as a purse.

Long stuff: demersal fish of the cod family (e.g. cod, haddock, whiting) and some other varieties such as hake and ling. The term was used to distinguish such species from flatfish.

Preparing **longlines** on Aldeburgh beach. Bath tubs are a convenient way of holding the lines to prevent tangling.

Look on: to inspect the first drift-net (nearest the boat), or even the first two or three, to see the quantity of herrings enmeshed and to assess whether it was worth starting to haul.

Loom: the glow of a lighthouse or lightship, on the horizon, before the light itself is actually seen. The word can be traced back to the late sixteenth century, when it had the general meaning of "to appear indistinctly".

Lop: a heavy swell on the sea. This definition ties in with early nineteenth century usage, when the word meant "water breaking in short, lumpy waves".

Louse-trap: the fine-toothed comb used to rake children's hair, in the search for head-lice.

Lousy: the word used to describe fish that were infested with parasites. Among the common ones noted were *Caligus curtus* (a species of sea louse) on cod, *Pontobdella muricata* (a type of leech) on roker and skate, and *Lernaeocera branchialis* (a species of copepod) on cod and whiting. The last-named infested the gills of the fish and was sometimes referred to as a **maggot** (q.v.).

Loves: the wooden racks/frames on the inside walls of **smokehouses** (q.v.) which supported the **speets** (q.v.) and **baulks** (q.v.) of fish to be cured. The word may be a variant of the French *louver/louvre*, in view of the fact that slats of wood were involved in the construction.

Lower landing: the wooden staging below the level of the fish market floor at Lowestoft onto which catches were once landed, before being passed up for display and sale (see the picture on page 180). This feature was the direct result of herrings being counted out by hand rather than being landed directly in baskets (which became standard practice after the Cran Measure Act of 1908). A lower landing-stage was needed for the effective handling of the baskets of counted herrings.

Lowestoft Revival (The): a period of religious fervour in the town, during the spring, summer and autumn of 1921, created by the preaching of a Baptist minister from Balham, London, the Rev. A. Douglas Brown. This man and his associates also had an influence on people in Great Yarmouth, as well as those dwelling in a number of Scottish fishing-ports – many of their itinerant crews and shore personnel carrying the message home with them when they returned after the autumn herring voyage.

Lowsterman: a fisherman from Lowestoft. The term takes account of local pronunciation.

Lucky boat: a term used (in Lowestoft particularly) of a fishing vessel that was a regular and prolific earner.

Lucky skipper: a description used of a successful master, who made good money largely by his expertise. There was an element of good fortune in fishing, but personal know-how and experience were the key factors. It is interesting to note that a number of big earners tended to refer to themselves as "lucky" – preferring to play down the level of personal skill involved.

Luff: the leading, or for'ad, edge of a sail.

Luff up: to bring a vessel up head to wind.

Lug: 1. A **becket(t),** (q.v.). There may be metaphorical usage at work here, in that a loop in a rope's end may be roughly comparable in appearance with the human ear. 2. The Lugworm (*Arenicola marina*), a polychaete of the Opheliidae family. It remains popular as bait and is dug from mudflats all round the British coast.

Lugger: a sailing drifter. By the time the people whose terminology is recorded in this book had begun work, the *lugger* (employing the rig described immediately below) had been long superseded by the *dandy* with its fore-and-aft sails – but the earlier term continued to be used. A typical length of vessel, during the late nineteenth century, would have been in the range of 50-60 feet.

Lugsail: a square sail of varying dimensions, set obliquely on a movable **yard** (q.v.). It is a transitional design between *square rig* and *fore-and-aft rig*.

Lumper: a fish market worker who unloaded catches from trawlers. The term is one which became increasingly used after World War II, but it has origins as far back as the end of the eighteenth century, when it meant "a labourer employed in loading and unloading cargoes, especially timber".

Lust(ed): list(ed). The derivation here would seem to be one of mispronunciation.

M

Maatjes: lightly pickled, high-quality herrings, without milt or roe in them – a Dutch speciality and word. The term is pronounced "madgies".

Mackerel herring-nets: herring nets that were made from heavier cotton than was usual and had thicker mesh-strands, like those on drift-nets, used for catching mackerel.

Mackerel livers: these were eaten either fried or raw by fishermen engaged on the annual migration to Newlyn, known as the **West'ard** (q.v.) voyage. If raw, they were simply put into an enamel mug, seasoned with salt, pepper and vinegar, and eaten like shellfish. Cornish mackerel were larger and of better quality than ones caught in the North Sea, and there was a belief current at one time among some fishermen in Great Yarmouth and Lowestoft that the species was a **dirty fish** (q.v.) – at least, as far as the North Sea was concerned. This resulted from the state of the gut and its contents, but there was also the idea that the dark flesh along the backbone (the swim-muscles) would poison the blood, if eaten – especially during the summer months.

Mackerel sky: *cirrocumulus* cloud(s) – small globular masses, which take the form of a series of lines with a rippled appearance. The formation is compared with a mackerel's skin and was usually regarded as a sign of approaching wet weather.

MAFF: see **Fish Labs**.

Maggies: Scottish fisher-girls.

Maggot(s): the parasitic copepod *Lernaeocera branchialis*, which infested the gills of members of the cod group of fish.

Main: 1. The mainland. The term was much applied to northern Scotland when the Shetland herring voyage was over and the boats worked southwards down the east coast. 2. The mainmast on a smack, and sometimes even its boom. 3. The mainsail. All three definitions obviously work on the principle of abbreviation.

Mainmast: the principal mast on a vessel. In the days of square rig, it was the middle one of the three. On the Lowestoft smacks and sailing drifters, it was the more for'ad of the two masts and was, in fact, sometimes referred to as the *foremast*.

Mainsail: the primary (and largest) sail rigged on the mainmast.

Maise: the hard roe (eggs) of the female herring.

Maisy: the term used of female herrings when they were close to spawning. It is hard to arrive at a possible derivation for the term – unless, at some stage, the spawn itself was thought similar in appearance to the granular effect of a bad skin rash and is a variant of *measly*.

Make round: an expression used to describe the turning of the tide.

Make up: 1. To finish a drifting voyage and get all the gear ready for checking and overhaul. 2 To recover from spawning and begin to fatten up (often used with reference to herrings).

Mand/maund: 1. A wicker basket holding about two and a half stones of herring. 2. A basket of similar dimensions used for handling sprats, which over the course of time became the unit by which a quantity of sprats was measured. The word was always pronounced *marnd* (*maand*) and probably derives from the from the Middle Low German or Middle Dutch *mande*. In Flemish, the word "maand" is still used for a basket.

Manil(l)a: hemp used in rope-making, deriving from the fibre of *Musa textilis*.

Margarine box: a wooden box, holding three stones of fish, which was used for packing herrings on board the drifters. The adoption of *margarines*, as they became known, made the landing process more efficient. Increasing use was made of them after the Second World War, with wood eventually being superseded by aluminium. The name derived from the fact that these boxes were similar in size and appearance to those in which packets of margarine left the manufacturers for the retail trade.

Market races: the day (usually Friday) on which driftermen's wives and relatives drew the weekly **allotment money** (q.v.) from the different companies' offices on Lowestoft fish market. The term matches the **Derby day** (q.v.) description referred to earlier.

Market suit: a fisherman's best wear, for changing into after docking at the end of a trip or a voyage.

Marks: physical features on shore, which were discernible out at sea and which served to give fishermen – especially **longshoremen** (q.v.) – reference-points on which to focus when at work. Church towers were a common feature used, as well as other prominent, high buildings, but in unbuilt areas even an individual and distinctive tree on the skyline might act as a marker.

Marl: 1. To join the forelock and beckett on a drift-net's **head-line** (q.v.). 2. To reinforce a section of fishing net by lacing a layer of meshes to it. The word derives from the Dutch *marlen*, meaning "to bind".

Marlinspike: a tapered wooden or iron spike, used to separate the strands of rope when **splicing** (q.v.) and also for forcing these through the loops formed as part of the process. The root of the first element of the word is the same as that specified in no. 2 immediately above.

Mash(es): meshes. The derivation is simply one of variant pronunciation.

Master-man: an expert; someone who was skilled in a particular aspect of fishing practice. For example: "He wuz a master-man at judgin' the colour o' the water for when herrin' were about."

Mate: the second-in-command on board a fishing-vessel, below the master or skipper. One of his main tasks on board ship, as well as relieving the skipper, was to take responsibility for the effective storage of catches.

Maternity bags: bags containing essential items of linen for women who were about to give birth (or who had just delivered). They usually contained a pair of sheets, night-dresses for the mother and child, and napkins. They were loaned to poor families by beneficent private individuals or by local organisations, such as churches and chapels.

Mat-fulls: herrings with milt or roe in them and not less than 9¼ inches long.

Matties: young, maturing herrings of not less than 9 inches in length. Both this term and the one immediately above were official categories in the Scottish **Crown Brand** (q.v.) process.

May Day: generally referred to by men who took part in the Spring trawling voyage to Padstow. The world-famous celebration which took place in the Cornish port (and still does), focused on perhaps the most singular of all hobby-horses, had a lasting effect on those who experienced it – becoming something they never forgot. Lowestoft had its own less well known rituals, largely child-centred, which included groups of local youngsters electing their respective May Queens and the boys blacking up their faces in the manner of *molly dancers*. The proceeds from door-to-door collections for pennies and ha'pennies were used to provide a special tea for the different groups of children in someone's house and, as the boys and girls gathered in the money, they sang a most distinctive song: *Climbing up the walls, / Knocking down the spiders, / Cabbages and turnips too. / Put them in an alleluiah saucepan / And then we'll have a real good stew!* The lyric would seem to have a passing reference to the traditional spring-cleaning of houses in the mention of spiders, while the word *alleluia* is likely to have been a variant of *aluminium* rather than a religious utterance.

Measured mile: a nautical mile, marked by beacons on shore, which was used for testing a steam (or diesel) vessel's maximum speed on its **trial trip** (q.v.).

Meg(s): The Megrim (*Lepidorhombus whiffiagonis*) – a flatfish mainly caught in waters south of the English Channel. It was sometimes passed off as *sole* in certain restaurants.

Melton: a high-quality, heavy woollen cloth, with a short nap, that was a popular material among fishermen (during the 1920s and 30s) to have overcoats made from. The association is with the town of Melton Mowbray, in Leicestershire, and the material was also in vogue with East Anglian farmworkers – especially horsemen.

Messenger: 1. An alternative name for the **warp** (q.v.) on a fleet of drift-nets. 2. A long wire strop, with a hook on one end, which was used for drawing the warps of an otter trawl towards the **towing-block** (q.v.) so that they could be fixed in place for towing.

Midsummer herring: full herring that were caught, during June and July, on the summer voyage to Shetland. They were usually very oily, with a tendency for the belly to tear if not carefully handled.

Mid-water boat: a trawler which fished areas of the sea at some distance from the home-port, but not to the extent of being far from it for weeks at a time as was the case with **distant-water** (q.v.) vessels.

Mid-water trawl: a trawl-net that was rigged to operate above the seabed, but at some distance down from the surface.

Milch(es): the soft roes, or sperm, of the male herring. The term was a medieval one originally, meaning "giving milk". The connection here is the colour and texture of the soft roes, especially close to spawning time.

Milford kit: 1. Twelve stones of trawl fish, in the Welsh port of Milford Haven. 2. The container which held this amount.

Milt: the soft roe of the male herring. At one time, the term applied to the spawn of male fishes generally.

Minesweeping: as early as 1907, Admiral Lord Charles Beresford had recognised the potential value of steam trawlers for minesweeping duties – the **otter trawl** (q.v.) gear itself not requiring a great deal of modification in order to carry out the work effectively. In both World Wars, British trawlers performed brave and effective service in the North Sea and also in foreign waters.

Ministry boats: research vessels belonging to the Ministry of Fisheries, which were based in Lowestoft. The town began its connection with fisheries research in 1902, with the establishment of a Marine Biological Association facility and the connection has continued since that time under a variety of different names (currently, CEFAS: Centre for Environment, Fisheries and Aquaculture Science). The first research vessel proper was the *George Bligh* (LO 309), a former **standard trawler** (q.v.), built in 1917 by Cochrane & Sons of Selby, which began its work in 1921. In the command of an ex-Naval or merchant-service man, this ship (and its successors) was partly crewed by former fishermen – who also worked the fishing-gear carried on board for the scientists, during the research trips at sea. A job on board a *Ministry boat* was highly regarded by Lowestoft men because of the security it offered and the good, regular wage it brought in.

Mission (The): The Royal National Mission to Deep Sea Fishermen. This was one of the great secular Christian agencies of the nineteenth century, being founded by Ebenezer Mather in 1881 to counter the unwholesome influence of the Dutch *grog ships* on English fishermen working in the trawling fleets on the Dogger Bank. Based originally at Gorleston, it remains active today in the larger surviving British fishing ports.

Mission hall: a place of worship for a non-denominational Nonconformist congregation, of evangelical practice, such as the one in St. George's Road, Pakefield (now used by The Society of Friends). Usually, there was no ordained minister to lead the people, but a local man who felt called to do such work and had sufficient Biblical knowledge to function effectively. This type of chapel was once to be found in operation in fishing communities throughout Great Britain.

Mission ship: the steam-powered successor to the smacks, as described immediately below. The *Joseph & Sarah Miles* (LO 175) was a well-known vessel in Lowestoft between the wars, carrying out its relief-work in the North Sea for fishermen in all kinds of need.

Mission smacks: ketch-rigged sailing trawlers belonging to the RNMDSF (the initials were commonly used), which initially operated out of the major English east coast fishing ports and kept the trawling fleets supplied with good quality (but cheap) tobacco, fishermen's comforts (such as woollen gloves and scarves) and religious reading material. All of this was intended to diminish the effect of the Dutch *grog ships* and attempt to bring some kind of civilising Christian influence to bear on men who often lived extremely bleak lives. When working with the fishing fleets (such as the Short Blue Fleet), the mission vessels also trawled on a semi-commercial basis, sending their catches to market by the cutters to boost the organisation's funds. Once the days of large-scale **fleeting** (q.v.) were over, the smacks diminished in number, but carried on providing a relieving service to fishermen in need at sea.

Mis-stay: to attempt to turn a sailing vessel about and not succeed in coming through the eye of the wind to complete the manoeuvre.

Mittens: fingerless woollen gloves which protected the wearer's palms, but which left his fingers free in the cause of dexterity. This was an important feature in colder weather when shooting and hauling nets, and also when gutting catches.

Mizzen: 1. The rear mast of a vessel, placed towards the stern. 2. The sail set on this mast. It was of particular importance on a steam drifter, to keep the boat steady while the nets were being shot.

Mizzen boom: the under-spar attached to the mizzen mast and sail.

Mixed fishing: a trawling term, used to describe fishing grounds where a variety of demersal species were caught.

Mock ollabuts: a Fleetwood term for flounders. There is a certain degree of irony at work here, the flounder being far inferior in size and flavour to its more illustrious cousin, the halibut (regarded by some people as being the finest of the flatfish). The word *ollabut* itself no doubt owes something to Lancashire pronunciation.

Molgogger: a portable fair-lead, with four vertical rollers and a horizontal one, which was set into a hole on a drifter's bow for the **warp** (q.v.) to run through when the nets were being hauled. The origin of the name is not known.

Mol(e)-jenny: an alternative name for the **molgogger**.

Money-box: the cod-end of a trawl. It was obviously given this name because that was the part of the gear where the earnings derived from.

Monk(s): the Angler Fish (*Lophius piscatorius*). The flesh of this voracious, bottom-dwelling predator is well flavoured and "monks' tails" have often been used as a substitute for scampi.

Monkey: a red and white chequered **buff** (q.v.), five nets from the **pole-end** (q.v.) on a fleet of drift-nets.

Monkey island: the signal bridge, or lookout platform, built on top of the wheelhouse of armed drifters and trawlers during World War I. This particular feature got its name from the climb required to reach it.

Monkey-knot: a braided and rounded knot in the end of a rope, which is intended to act as weight if the rope is thrown for any distance (e.g. from a vessel to the quayside). A monkey-knot, properly made, will enable a rope to carry through the air up to a distance of twenty yards or more.

Monkey triple: a three-cylinder marine steam engine, made by Elliott & Garrood of Beccles, in which the intermediate cylinder sat on top of the high pressure and low pressure ones. This was supposed to give the machinery the appearance of a monkey sitting on top of a barrel organ, hence the name. Monkey triples were very highly rated as a means of propulsion on the steam drifters, because they took up less space in the engine-room than the **out-length** (q.v.) ones, were economical in their use of coal, and had a large and extremely effective flywheel.

Monkfish: the Angler Fish (*Lophius piscatorius*), as above (five entries) – not the Angel Ray (*Squatina squatina*). The tail section of this species was once used as a scampi substitute, but has since become fashionable in the restaurant trade as a dish in its own right.

Monkey's fist: the monkey-knot, as above. The knot itself does have a passing resemblance to a fist, simian or otherwise.

Moorlog: fossilised trees of the Mesolithic period (usually the trunk and root system), lumps of which were often trawled up on the Dogger Bank. The term may be loosely analogous with "marsh log", or "bog oak" even, and the substance itself is evidence of the land-bridge which once joined Britain to the European mainland and which disappeared at the time of the last glacial ice-melt.

Mother Love's Ointment: see **Mrs. Love's Ointment** below.

Mother ship: a trawler or drifter in charge of a company's **fleeting** (q.v.) operation, whereby a number of vessels fished co-operatively. The skipper of the *mother ship* (usually, a man of long experience at sea) directed both the fishing and the transport of catches to market.

Motor: a petrol, or diesel, engine that was fitted to a fishing vessel.

Motor-smack: a sailing trawler that had been converted to diesel propulsion. There were a number of these working out of Lowestoft in the years before World War Two, with some of them continuing after the conflict was over. *Olsen's Fisherman's Nautical Almanack* for 1937 records nineteen of them registered in the port, with twelve belonging to three associated companies: W.H. Podd Ltd., Diesel Trawlers Ltd. and Inshore Trawlers Ltd. By 1967 only one such vessel, the *Helping Hand* (LT 1239), was still in operation.

Mould-loft: an upper space, in a shipyard, where the templates for a vessel's hull construction were made.

Moulds: softwood templates, the shape of the frames in a vessel's hull.

Mount (The): a wooden lookout tower which once stood at the entrance to Lowestoft fish market and from which local boys would watch for vessels returning to port. Once they had identified a boat, they would go to crew members' homes and inform the wives – usually in the hope of receiving some small reward for bringing news of the husbands' return. See also, **Run for a penny.**

Mousing: a twine whipping round a hook, to prevent it coming out of an eye.

Mrs. Love's Ointment: a salve made by a local woman in Lowestoft (wife of a carpenter, who lived at 60 Denmark Road), which fishermen used to protect their hands against the ravages of salt water. It was said to be very effective and was, of course, made from a "secret recipe". **Mother Love's Ointment** was another version of the name and the product was sold in a handful of the smaller, back-street shops.

Mud gulleys: the drowned river valleys of the Dogger Bank area, which had once formed the "land-bridge" with continental Europe, before becoming submerged at the time of the last glacial ice-melt 8-10,000 years ago. Productive trawl-fishing for demersal species was often to be had along them.

Mud herrings: inshore herrings caught off Mersea Island, in Essex. These were not very highly rated in either Great Yarmouth or Lowestoft.

Muddly: mild and moist weather, especially that at times when south-westerly winds prevailed. The word may possibly have been a composite one originally, deriving from *muggy* (re temperature and humidity) and *muddy* (re poor light).

Muldoon(y): a whale. Fishermen sometimes applied the term to dolphins and porpoises. It would appear to have Irish origins, but is difficult to attach to the Gaelic *Maoldúin* – name of an early chieftain in what is now County Fermanagh.

Mull(s): 1. The outer part of the mouth of rays and skate. 2. The lumps of flesh on a ray's body between the backbone and the wings. Many of the fishermen rated these highly for their eating qualities.

Muster: the term used of a lifeboat crew gathering for a launch.

Muzzled: the term used for when a longline's **snood** (q.v.) had become wrapped around a conger eel's jaws after the fish had been hooked.

N

Neat's foot oil: an extract from the hooves of cattle, which was applied to leather articles to retain suppleness and give water-proofing qualities. It was a popular agent among fishermen as a dressing for sea boots. The word *neat* derives from the Old English *nēat*, meaning "cattle", and remained in common use until the nineteenth century – even surviving into the twentieth. It was customary at one time in both Norfolk and Suffolk to refer to a cowshed as a *neat'us* (i.e. "neat house").

Needles: small hake. This term was used in Fleetwood and probably referred to the species' fine, pointed teeth.

Net a boat: the term used of an arrangement whereby steam drifter owners allowed second parties to provide the gear for a herring voyage and to take a certain percentage of the profits as the reward for their investment. This helped to spread the expense incurred in financing fishing ventures, as well as the risk if the voyage proved to be unprofitable.

Net-chamber: a long, two-storey shed, where fishing nets were repaired and stored. Repairs were usually done on the upper floor, which had no internal partitions and where the nets could be spread out. The lower floor was arranged in compartments and storage bays, where various items of gear were kept. The *chamber* element of the term, deriving from the Old French *chambre*, had long tended to be used of first-floor bedrooms in English houses.

Net-knife: a bill-like blade on the end of a long pole, used for cutting rope(s) from a fouled propeller.

Net-roller: a wooden roller fixed to the side of a drifter's hold, which facilitated the shooting and hauling of nets.

Net-rope: the head-rope, or cork-line, on a drift net.

Net-rope man: the crew member on a drifter responsible for shooting the **lint** (q.v.). The term was probably a hang-over from an earlier period, because in the steam and diesel eras it was the **hawseman** (q.v.) and **waleman** (q.v.) who shot the net-rope.

Net-stower: the crew member on a steam-drifter responsible for shooting the **back-rope** (q.v.). Again, the term is probably a survivor from an earlier period, because stowing the nets after a haul was a shared duty.

Net(t) earnings: the money earned by a fishing vessel (at the end of a trip, or voyage) after all the running expenses had been met.

Nettle: a twisted length of wire and twine, used to hold a pin in place. The strands were twisted together, whipped at the ends and rove through the head of the pin. The term was a variant pronunciation of *knittle*.

Nickey boats: a general term for Cornish fishing vessels of the sailing variety, using a lugsail rig. The term is said to have derived from "Nicholas", a common name among Cornish fishermelation. Isle of Man luggers were also called *nickeys*, because they adopted the lugsail rig from Cornish boats round about the middle of the nineteenth century.

Night-man: a substitute fisherman on steam drifters, who stood in for a sick regular crew member during the autumn Home Fishing. He was called a "night man" because the drifters usually operated at night and returned to port the following day. Only an insufficient catch would cause them to stay out an extra night.

Night-smoker: a fish-curer who tended a **smokehouse** (q.v.) during the night. This was a job usually associated with the large fish-processing companies in Great Yarmouth and Lowestoft, which were producing cured herrings (especially kippers) on a grand scale.

Nip: the term used of a trawler turning to port or starboard while towing its gear.

Nipped: the term used for a vessel and its crew being arrested by a fisheries patrol craft for fishing inside a **limit-line** (q.v.). It is obviously a variant of "pinched", a common expression at one time for being arrested by the police.

Nipper: a male net-store worker who squeezed the excess tar out of freshly treated drift-net **warps** (q.v.).

Norsel: a length of twine which linked the top and bottom ropes on a drift-net with the oddy. There were between 180 and 190 norsels on the **head-rope** (q.v.) and 90 or so on the **back-rope** (q.v.).

Norsel up: to put the norsels in place on a drift-net.

North Sea pheasants: herrings. The term is a metaphorical one, which seeks to elevate the most commonly eaten fish of its time in terms of status. To compare it with game (when game was largely eaten by the "upper classes") does this. In terms of flavour, however, the herring, in all its many forms, fresh and cured, was superb.

North Sea sauce: a mixture of seawater, mustard and malt vinegar, used as a condiment with cooked fish (being especially popular on the drifters to accompany fried herrings). It was generally reckoned to have been at its best when given about a week to mature.

Numbered Fleet (The): the fleet of steam drifters working out of Great Yarmouth before the First World War (and registered in the port), belonging to the Smith's Dock Trust Company Ltd. of North Shields. There were thirty-seven of these altogether and they had no individual names of the conventional kind. They were simply numbered from one onwards, the numbers being spelt out as *Three, Twenty-three* etc.

Nurse: the Larger-spotted Dogfish (*Scyliorhinus stellaris*). It was given this name because of reputed healing secretions which exuded from the skin. Some fishermen would apply a piece of dogfish skin to a wound before bandaging it over. The term *nurse* was also sometimes applied to the Lesser-spotted Dogfish (*Scliorhinus caniculus*).

Nurse-skins: both species of dogfish referred to immediately above had rough skins, which were sometimes used as an abrasive material to rub down and clean the deck-planks of sailing smacks.

O

Oarsman: see **Hawseman**. The word is a variant pronunciation, largely caused by dropping the initial h.

October full: the October full moon. This was always reckoned to be the best time for catching herrings on the autumn Home Fishing.

Oddie/oddy: the reinforced meshes at the top and bottom of a drift-net.

Offal: 1. Fish guts and other waste. 2. Condemned fish, which was unfit for sale. 3. Trawlfish that wasn't classed as **prime** (q.v.). The term derives from the Middle Dutch word *afval*, meaning "animal guts and waste"

Oil: to treat drift-nets (mainly those for catching mackerel) with linseed oil.

Oil-bangers: lightships with oil-fired lights.

Oil factory: the herring reduction plant at Great Yarmouth, which was built in the 1930s to convert surplus herring to fish oil in times of **glut** (q.v.).

Oily frock: a fisherman's oilskin smock. The word *frock*, as used here, goes back well into the medieval period and has the meaning of "a long garment with large open sleeves." It was free of any specific female connotations.

Oily skirt: a full-length over-garment, sometimes with an integral bibbed top, worn by Scottish **gutting-girls** (q.v.) to act as a barrier against herring grease and scales.

Old man: the term traditionally used of the commander or master of any type of vessel at sea.

Ollabuts: Halibut (*Hippoglossus*). This term was used in Fleetwood and reflects Lancashire dialect pronunciation. See also, **Mock ollabuts**.

Olsen's: the abbreviated form usually given to *Olsen's Fisherman's Nautical Almanack*, published originally in Grimsby in 1876 and transferred to E.T.W. Dennis & Sons Ltd. of Scarborough at some point. This most useful compendium of maritime information was highly valued by fishermen (especially skippers and mates) and was first published in 1876 by Ole Theodor Olsen (1838-1925), a Norwegian mariner who had spent a number years on board British merchant ships. On coming ashore, he settled in Grimsby and, in addition to the publication cited here, produced his *Piscatorial Atlas of the North Sea, English and St. George's Channels* (1883) – a formative work based on material collected by questionnaires given out to Humberside fishermen.

On a living: a term used of productive and profitable fishing at any time of the year. It tended to be applied rather more to **trawling** (q.v.) than to **drifting** (q.v.) and was even used as a form of description as to the viability of particular grounds, according to the season and to local conditions of weather and tide.

On the bone: a description used of the way that **white fish** (q.v.) was largely sold (locally, at least) in both fishmongers' and fish-friers' shops before the Second World War – in other words, unfilleted. Commercial filleting first appeared during the early 1920s, with Jim Eunson of Aberdeen being accredited with its development, and within a few years the practice was being widely adopted in the major trawling centres such as Hull and Grimsby. Lowestoft, however, remained a whole-fish port at this time and continued as such until fishing returned to normal after the Second World War.

On the cant: an expression used of a sailing smack under way in a stiff breeze. The vessel used to **heel over** (q.v.) and move at an angle through the water (not unlike a yacht) – a position that was held for as long as the conditions which caused it prevailed. This shift from the perpendicular could cause problems down below in the galley, and more than one man who had worked as cook on board sailing trawlers made reference to the difficulty of frying fish in a pan when the fat had run to one side of the utensil and stayed there! The word *cant* itself, in this case, simply means a deflexion from the perpendicular.

On-the-door gear: an otter trawl, without the refinement of **bridles** (q.v.). The net was joined to the doors by much shorter **legs** (q.v.).

On the quarter: with the wind astern, either to port or starboard.

One-and-one: a piece of fried fish and a penny's worth of chips. This was a standard serving in fish-and-chip shops during the 1920s and was considered to make an adequate (if not lavish!) meal.

One man at sea (eight on shore): a common saying at one time, used to illustrate the amount of employment created by fishing. Whether the arithmetic had been properly worked out to establish the ratio of fishermen to shore-workers is debatable, but there is no doubt that a fishing fleet of any size in an individual port did create a large body of workers in associated activities – from work connected with the construction and repair of vessels, with the manufacture and maintenance of gear, with the provisioning of craft, and with the handling, processing and transportation of catches.

Oosties: fishermen from Ostend.

Open: the term used of a company (or an individual merchant) beginning to buy and trade in fish in a port previously unvisited.

Open arseholes: Beadlet Sea-anemones (*Actinia equina*). These were commonly trawled up in parts of the North Sea, with a good degree of colour variation in evidence. This most graphic of descriptions refers especially to the red variety.

Ossel: another term for **norsel** (q.v.). It is possible that either word could be a variant of the other, but there is no way of ascertaining which came first – if, indeed, there is precedence in the matter.

Other side (the): Holland or Belgium (particularly the former). Herrings were sometimes landed at fish markets in these countries, across the North Sea, if a better price was to be had there than on the home market. During the early 1960s, Skipper Ernest ("Jumbo") Fiske had a record catch on board, which would have won the **Prunier Trophy** (q.v.), but he was ordered by his company to land in Ijmuiden.

Otter gear: see Otter trawl immediately below.

Otter trawl: a triangular bag-net, pulled along the seabed, whose mouth was kept open at the upper extremities by two, heavy wooden **doors**

(q.v.), which acted as paravanes and were secured to the vessel by wire cables (rope, originally). It was a major development in fishing technique during the last quarter of the nineteenth century.

Out: out of work; unemployed.

Out-length triple: a large triple-expansion marine steam engine, with all three cylinders in line. A particularly fine example can be seen in the *Lydia Eva* (YH 89), the last surviving steam **drifter-trawler** (q.v.) in this country. The vessel is now run as a herring-fishery museum by an independent charitable trust and may be visited from April to October at Hall Quay, Great Yarmouth. The engine unit was made by the Great Yarmouth engineering firm of Crabtree Ltd.

Out o': the expression used to describe a particular fishing-port where fishermen were based on either a short-term basis or for a much longer period of time. Thus one man might say, "We were workin' out o' Newlyn, fishin' for mackerel" and another "Yeah, I sailed out o' Fleetwood for nearly thirty year altogether".

Outrigger: a spar projecting from the stern of a boat which helped to support a dipping-lug mizzen sail.

Outside: deep water; well out from land. The term originated from the specific meaning of being out beyond the coastal sandbanks, such as the Barnard Sand, the Holm Sand and the Scroby.

Outside mending: 1. A term used for the repair of herring nets carried out by beatsters in their own homes (the nets were delivered by horse and cart and, later, by lorries). The kitchen was a common place for this to be done, with the hook set on the wall near the window. Another place where the mending was commonly done was the garden shed – sometimes by retired fishermen, as well as their wives. 2. The repair of drift-nets which was sometimes carried out, during the summer, on the North Denes at Lowestoft, opposite certain of the net-stores. This practice gave the beatsters more space than was available inside and they enjoyed being out in the fresh air – especially when handling nets impregnated with jellyfish dust.

Overdays: herrings which were kept on a drifter overnight, either salted and iced, or left untreated. This was always done in the event of an insufficient catch, when the vessel would remain out at sea another night in the hope of getting a better haul. *Overdays* were always kept separate from the fresher fish on board and were declared by their name when landed at market.

Overhand knot: the knot that secured the tie around a drift-net at the end of a voyage and indicated that it was beyond repair (either because it was very old or because it had been badly damaged by dogfish). It was the simplest of knots to tie (the making of a loop by crossing the ends of the string or twine), and this was why it was used. There was no point in forming a more complex knot for a condemned net.

Over-overs: herrings that were two days old and which had been salted and iced on board ship. This practice usually indicated poor catches, with the drifter staying out a third night in order to make a profitable trip.

Over-run: to steam, sail or row (depending on the size and type of vessel) up and down a fleet of drift-nets or (more particularly) a set of longlines, to check up on the quantity of fish being caught.

Overtail: the specific number of twelve herrings, by which the **long hundred** (q.v.) increased from 120 to 132. *Tail* could have the sense either of an imposed payment or be a variant of *tally*.

P

P-boat: a small, fast, destroyer-type naval vessel used for patrol duties during the First World War.

Padstow shovels: large cuckoo rays (*Raia naevus*). These were commonly caught on the Cornish fishing grounds, off Padstow, during the spring season for soles. The shape of any ray may be compared with that of the type of shovel which had a curved and pointed blade.

Paid off: the term used for when a **share fisherman** (q.v.) drew the money owed to him by his employer, at the end of a voyage.

Painted ladies: the name given to **kippers** (q.v.) which had had their colour enhanced by **annatto** (q.v.) vegetable dye. This was done by some curers to make their product more eye-catching for the customer. It added nothing to the quality of the fish; in fact, it detracted from it.

Painter: a rope mooring-line used on small craft. The word derives from the Old French *penteur*, which was a rope running down from a masthead to gunwale or deck.

Pair-fishing: a term used for two craft pulling a **trawl** (q.v.) or **seine** (q.v.) together. The kind of gear usually employed was the mid-water trawl, which operated somewhere between the surface and the seabed and aimed at catching pelagic fish such as herring and mackerel.

Paralysed: a term used of trawl gear getting smashed up, usually on a very rough seabed (such as the shale outcrops, found offshore at Padstow) or on some underwater obstacle such as a wreck.

Parent ship: see **Mother ship**.

Parliament: a beach company shed, or a room within the same. As with **Court** (q.v.), there is an element of grandification here, but probably with a greater degree of ironic humour.

Part(ed): a term used when the **net-rope** (q.v.) on a drift-net broke, or when the **warp** (q.v.) did the same. The word was also used in reference to one or both warps on a trawl breaking.

Patches: a Fleetwood term for small Blonde Rays (*Raja brachyura*).

Patrolling: maritime scrutiny for enemy activity at sea undertaken by British steam fishing-craft in both World Wars of the twentieth century. The drifters and trawlers, with their crews, provided a ready-made naval force for service in the North Sea, the English Channel, the Atlantic Approaches and the Mediterranean. Lowestoft became the great hub of the Royal Naval Patrol Service in the Second World War and the national memorial to men killed in the service, as well as a museum dedicated to them, may be seen in the town's Belle Vue Park-Sparrow's Nest Gardens area. See also, **Harry Tate's Navy**.

Paying trip: a profitable trawling trip.

Pawl: a metal bar which engaged with the teeth on a ratchet-wheel. The word possibly derives from the Low Dutch *pal*, meaning "immobile" or "fixed".

Pay off: 1. A term used of a vessel veering to either port or starboard, as result of wind strength and/or tidal action. 2. To receive the money due to crew members at the end of a drifting **voyage** (q.v.), if the vessel had made a profit.

Pea-bellies: a Great Yarmouth term for Lowestoft fishermen. It goes back into the eighteenth century when the Sea Pea plant (*Lathyrus japonicus*), which grew on the Lowestoft *denes*, formed part of local people's diet. The term, originally, had a derisory quality about it, reflecting the traditional rivalry between the two towns – this, itself, already four hundred years old by 1750 and caused largely by the determination of the Norfolk town to exercise control of its neighbour's maritime trade (an unsuccessful area of activity, as things turned out).

Pearl twists: double-stranded, heavy cotton **drift-nets** (q.v.). These were very effective at catching herrings, but hard on the fishermen's hands.

Peck: 1. A round wooden tray on which **longlines** (q.v.) were coiled. The term may have arisen because the coiled lines formed a mass about the same size as a two-gallon bucket. 2. An Imperial-measure capacity of two gallons by volume, when applied to dry goods – and there were four pecks to the *bushel*. Shrimps were always sold by the *peck* on a fish market and by the *pint* in the shops.

Ped: 1. A tall wicker basket. This Middle English word was the origin of *pedlar* – someone who travelled round from place to place, selling goods carried in a basket. 2. A willow hoop, with a canvas base, on which **longlines** (q.v.) were coiled. Given the identical nature of the function, there may be a possible connection here with the word *peck* as outlined immediately above.

Peg anchor: a small anchor, which was used to secure the main mooring anchor employed in **Danish seine-net** (q.v.) fishing.

Pellet(s): buff(s). The generally spherical shape of the **buff** (q.v.) gave rise to the term here. Pellet itself derives from the Latin *pilotta*, a diminutive of *pila*, meaning "a ball".

Pendant: a rope to which a tackle is fixed and which therefore hangs down. The word derives from the Latin *pendere*, meaning "to hang down".

Pennant: a wire strop on Vigneron Dahl trawling gear which linked the bridle and the warp and allowed continuous winching in of the gear. The word is a corruption of "independent", because this particular piece of equipment was not integral with either the otter door or the warp, but simply served as a connecting agent between the two.

Penny-stamps: very small plaice – analogous, more or less with **butterflies** (q.v.).

Perk-boards: cross boards, or planks, fitted into the top of a steam drifter's hold, on which crew members stood while hauling in the nets. The first element is a variant of *perch* and is retained in East Anglian dialect with regard to chicken-houses, where the cross-bars on which the hens roost are still referred to as *perks*. Nor should it be forgotten that in the late medieval period, in East Anglia, the rood beam in churches was often called "the perk".

Perks: perk-boards.

Peter's fish: the John Dory, as previously referred to. The term was also applied to other fish which had a single dark spot on either side of the body. Thus the Haddock (*Melanogrammus aeglefinus*), the Red Sea Bream (*Pagellus bogaraveo*) and the Bib or Pout (*Trisopterus luscus*) enter the classification. Legend has it that these four fish were the ones taken from the net by the apostle after the miraculous draught of fishes (John 21. 1-13).

Pick: a boathook. It was the curved prong which gave rise to this name.

Pickle: 1. To cure, or preserve, gutted herrings in salt. 2. The solution of salt and herring juices which formed in the barrel(s) as an essential element in the Scotch Cure process. See also, **Blood pickle**.

Pickles: Scotch Cure herrings.

Pickling-plots: areas of land on which Scottish gutting-girls and coopers worked, producing pickled herrings.

Piece: a term used in **Klondyking** (q.v.) for a quantity of herrings left over after packing (this usually resulted from there being more fish than boxes to put them in).

Pierhead paintings: a term devised and used (much later than the period in which such artwork was produced) for pictures of local fishing craft – particularly steam drifters and sailing trawlers. These "side-on" studies of individual vessels were produced largely by local amateur artists for vessel-owners and crew members (especially skippers) and were very much a feature of the Lowestoft-Great Yarmouth fishing industry from about 1890 up until the outbreak of the First World War. The 1920s and 30s saw a continuation of the process, but it was greatly reduced in scale and there is no doubt that the heyday of these pictures coincided with the maximum level of fishing activity and prosperity. Executed mainly in oils (though one or two operatives preferred gouache), they vary in their level of competence or naivety – depending on how the work is viewed. Among the main exponents of the style, the following men may be mentioned: G.V. Burwood, Fred Love, John (Jack) Gregory, George Race, Ernest Tench, Tom Swan and Kenneth Luck – the last-named working in tandem with photographer, Claude Mowle. The list is not exclusive and other notable talents existed. The whole "school", if it may be so termed, was one of the more interesting cultural aspects of the local fishing industry.

Pigeon-feed: 1. To sprinkle salt lightly on herrings or sprats. 2. To feed a steam vessel's furnace with small amounts of coal.

Pikey: a marine worm which lived in a tube of sand grains – probably either *Sabellaria alveolata* or *Pectinaria koreni*. These polychaetes provided good feed for plaice and other species. The word itself is almost certainly a variant of *pipey* – a reference to the tubes (or pipes) in which the creatures lived.

Pilcher: the Pilchard (*Sardina pilchardus*). The word is a simple mispronunciation and the species was mainly encountered on the fishing voyages made to Cornwall.

Pilot: an old, experienced hand taken on a voyage to advise the crew either on a new method of fishing (new to them, that is) or on how to work previously unvisited grounds (which were known to him).

Ping-pongs: haddocks. No explanation can be offered as to derivation.

Pining: the pickling-process in **Scotch cure** (q.v.), whereby the salt and herring juices combined and blended. This took about ten days in all and, while it was going on, the layers of fish in the barrels shrunk. This "wasting away" probably gave rise to the term.

Pink shrimp: the Aesop Prawn (*Pandalus montagui*) – which turned pink, when boiled for eating. This species was very much a staple product of the Great Yarmouth (and Gorleston) longshore fishermen and proved very popular with summer visitors to the seaside. The rival town of Lowestoft was known for its **brown shrimps** (q.v.).

Pipey: pikey. This term was probably the original one, referring as it does to the tubes of sand grains in which the worms lived.

Pitch: 1. The dipping-down and consequent rise of a vessel's bow in heavy seas. 2. The noise made by a vessel's screw or propeller.

Plaice-rash: irritation to the hands caused when gutting plaice and resulting from small shells in the gut itself.

Plank: a basket-maker's bench, on which he sat and worked.

Platten: a canvas pad made of three or four individual thicknesses, which was tied to the rail of a smack to prevent the warp from chafing during hauling. In the sense of this artefact being flat and placed under pressure when in operation, it may perhaps be compared with the plate of a printing-press. It would certainly seem to derive from the French *plat*, meaning "flat".

Play the wag: to play truant from school. The term is one that dates from the middle of the nineteenth century and was in general use at one time. The word *wag* itself originally meant "a mischievous boy" and may have had its derivation in *waghalter*, meaning "someone likely to swing in an executioner's noose". The transference from serious crime to a lesser offence, in the cause of making a joke, is entirely feasible – and it is interesting that *truant* itself (possibly deriving from the Gaelic *truaghan*, meaning "wretched") was a word once used in pre-industrial times to describe a vagabond or beggar.

Pleasure-trip: a fishing trip made by a young lad, on either drifter or trawler, in the company of his father, a relative or family friend. Whether it was pleasurable or not, depended on a number of things – particularly the degree of seasickness experienced!

Plonk: a slang term (current during the mid-twentieth century, to describe putting an object down heavily), which was used for selecting a place to fish and getting the gear over the side of the boat. The word applied more to **trawling** (q.v.) than to **drifting** (q.v.).

Plug-hatches: tapered hatch covers on insulated fish-holds. The inner covers below the coamings were made of wood, with a cork interior. This type of hatch cover was usually fitted to distant-water trawlers working grounds off Iceland and in the White Sea and Barents Sea and was designed to make a tight seal against penetration by salt water from the heavy seas encountered.

Poach: to fish inside a limit-line, thereby contravening both local and national regulations. The transference from the illegal taking of game is one which is easily understood.

Pockets: tapering spaces at the entrance of a beam trawl's **cod-end** (q.v.), which formed a fish trap.

Poke: 1. The length of a Danish seine net from the ground-rope and the head-line to the extremity of the cod-end. 2. A cloth money-bag.

Pole-end: the first drift-net shot and the last one hauled. The term derives from the type of marker-buoy used to indicate the **fleet's** (q.v.) extreme end. See also, **Dan**.

Pole-ending: stealing herrings from a vessel's furthest nets. With a fleet of drift-nets being anything between a mile and a half and two miles long, this kind of subterfuge could go unnoticed.

Pollack whiting: the Pollack (*Pollachius pollachius*) – a species caught on trawling voyages in Cornish waters and the Irish Sea, which was not highly rated by East Anglian fishermen on account of the dryness of its flesh.

Pollard(s): bollard(s). The word is a simple mispronunciation.

Pooling: a system devised for stabilising and controlling the price of herrings in the period immediately after the Second World War. It worked in the following way: all vessels that landed their catches up to a certain time each working-day went into a particular pool and received the average price realised across all of the individual sales that had taken place.

Poop one: the term used of a vessel catching a following sea and being swamped. The word *poop* derives from the Latin *puppis*, meaning "the stern of a ship", which gives perfect sense to the term here.

Pork of the sea: a term sometimes used of the Herring (*Clupea harengus*), largely during the nineteenth century. It does not have a specific East Anglian connotation and may be taken to reflect the fine eating-qualities of the fish, as well as its general availability.

Pork-line: a strop on a trawl that ran from the cod-end becket(t) up to the head-line and was used to hoist the cod-end when hauling was in progress. It was similar in purpose to the **lazy deckie** (q.v.).

Port missionary: a representative of the British Sailors' Society, who also supervised activity at **The Bethel** (q.v.) and who often had the unenviable task of informing families of the loss at sea of near-relatives.

Potchet platters: earthenware soup/cereal bowls – a standard item among a vessel's utensils. The word *potchet* may be a variant, or derivative, of "pot-earth".

Pots: basket-traps of varying size and shape, made from cane and wicker, which were baited and placed on the seabed to catch crabs and lobsters. Later models used plastic mesh stretched over wooden or metal frames.

Pound: a compartment on deck, or in the hold, in which fish was stored. The word probably derives from the Old English *pyndan*, meaning "to shut in" or "impound".

Pound-boards: planks used to divide deck or hold space into storage compartments. Often these slotted into grooved metal uprights.

Poundage: a percentage payment per £100 net earnings made to trawler skippers and mates (and often to other crew members) on top of their wages.

Practice money: payments made to lifeboat crews for practice launches.

Prick: 1. To affix kippers to baulks prior to smoking. 2. To push the end of a rope through an eye.

Cromer fisherman Kelly Harrison cleans and rebaits a **pot** aboard the **crab-boat** that he worked with his brother..

Prick on: to affix kippers to **baulks** (q.v.). The term is an appropriate one because the fish were impaled on tenter-hooks, which were set in pairs (one pair per fish) and spaced at regular intervals across the length of the baulk.

Prime (fish): sole, turbot, brill (*Scophthalmus rhombus*) and halibut. The term was applied to species which made the most money at market – their destination mainly being into the restaurant trade either in England or on the European mainland.

Prunier Trophy: an award made annually from 1936-66, by the proprietors of the famous London fish restaurant, to the drifter which caught the largest single **shot** (q.v.) of herrings during the East Anglian autumn season. This was done to promote interest in herrings and raise the profile of seafood. The trophy itself was a grey, polished stone sculpture (about a foot high) of a hand grasping a herring and it can now be seen in the Lowestoft and East Suffolk Maritime Museum. The winning vessel was also given a special vane to fly at the masthead for the year following its success.

Pud: a Fleetwood term for a Lowestoft fisherman.

Puddly water: oily water at sea, which indicated the presence of herring. There is an obvious connection here with *puddle*, in the sense of the water being less than clear. The word puddle itself is a diminutive of the Old English *pudd*, meaning "a ditch".

Puffer: a small steam vessel which carried goods from port to port on the west coast of Scotland. The term conjures up thoughts of Para Handy and *The Vital Spark*.

Pull up: to clean drift-nets after hauling had finished, in order to have them ready for the next **shoot** (q.v.).

Pull out: to come to the end of a fishing voyage, which was often indicated by diminishing catches. Thus, the owner of a vessel might say to the skipper, "I reckon you're just about pulled out, dun't you?"

Pulling-and-sailing lifeboat: a craft propelled by oar and sail, which was also double-ended in the sense of there being no difference between bow and stern. This added greatly to the versatility and handling qualities of the vessel. The more usual term was **Sailing-and-pulling** (q.v.).

Punch: to steam against the wind. The image is very much one of physical effort and battling against the elements.

Punt: a longshore boat, propelled either by oars or dipping lugsails fore and aft. The term is one very much associated with Southwold and it derives from the Low German *pünte* or the Middle Dutch *ponte*, meaning "a ferryboat".

Pup(s): small spur dogfish. The analogy with the offspring of man's favourite domestic animal is obvious.

Push-net: a small net, rigged on a T-shaped frame, for pushing along in shallow water and catching shrimps. During the heyday of the traditional British seaside holiday, from the Victorian period onwards, cheap versions of the device were commonly sold to visitors in many resorts as a novelty or plaything.

Q

Qualmy: queasy; feeling sick. As one particular long-time fisherman once remarked to the writer: "I wuz allus qualmy the first day or two at sea." The usage reflects the original, early sixteenth century meaning of *qualm*.

Quant: a long pole used to punt barges and wherries along, either when there was no wind or when there was little room for manoeuvre. The word perhaps derives from the Latin *contus*, meaning "a long pole or staff." The wherry proper was the classic single-sail, trading craft of the Norfolk Broads.

Quanted: the term used of a vessel being propelled by a quant.

Quarantine flags: small dabs and plaice hung to dry, prior to being eaten, on trawler mizzen booms (especially on Dutch and Belgian vessels). The analogy here is with the number of signal-flags required to indicate that a boat was in quarantine.

Quarter: one of the four cardinal compass-points or directions (north, south, east and west).

Quarter-rope/strop: the rope used to lift an otter or beam trawl's ground-rope inboard. See **Leach-line**.

Quarters: those areas of an **otter trawl** (q.v.) where the upper wings meet the head-line, or where the lower wings meet the bosom.

Queen/queenie: the Queen Scallop (*Chlamys opercularis*). This was a valued by-catch among the crew on trawlers because of its good eating qualities.

R

Raft: a flat-bottomed skiff, used by painters to reach vessels lying in dock and requiring maintenance work on the hulls.

Rafty: a term used to describe damp, raw, misty weather and always pronounced as "rarfty".

Rag mats: mats, or small rugs, made from cutting up pieces of cloth into strips and then pulling them through a woven hessian backcloth (or a piece of sacking) with the aid of a special tool. They were sufficiently functional in people's homes, but soon became dirty. Some of the men who worked on board the Lowestoft **smacks** (q.v.) used to take these mats to sea with them, tie them securely to one end of a slender rope, make fast the other end to something near the stern of the vessel, throw them overboard and let the action of the sea clean them. It was customary to do this, usually, on the outward leg of a trawling trip.

Rail: the gunwale.

Rail-roller: a wooden roller fitted to a drifter's gunwale to prevent nets and ropes from fouling and chafing.

Rake: the deviation from the perpendicular of a vessel's mast (a use first recorded in 1815). A slight "lean" forward on the mizzen was an unmistakable feature of Lowestoft drifters, both sail and steam.

Rammies: 1. Ramsgate fishermen. 2. Ramsgate smacks. It was men from this Kentish port, as well as from Hastings, whose migration to Lowestoft during the second half of the nineteenth century was instrumental in founding the trawling industry there.

Ransacker: a man who checked and rigged drift-nets. A medieval drift-net consisted of four sections, or *ranns*, which were laced together to form the net. *Sacker* is a variant of "seeker", deriving from the Old English *sēćan* or the Old Norse *sœkja*.

Ransacking bag: a bag taken on board herring drifters, which contained equipment for mending nets.

Rape: a term used in Lowestoft and Great Yarmouth for the **foot-rope** (q.v.) on a Scotch mackerel-net (i.e. one that was made of fine cotton as opposed to coarser thread or hemp). The word most likely derived from Old English *rāp*, meaning "a rope".

Rats: there is nothing metaphorical or mysterious in this entry. The Brown, or Grey, Rat (*Rattus norvegicus*) was a fact of life on fishing vessels of all kinds. Levels of infestation varied, but were particularly noticeable on craft which had been laid up for any length of time before being brought back into use. The most notorious vessels in Lowestoft for the rodents' profusion were the **Crown boats** (q.v.). "Rats forever!" one of the writer's respondents once remarked, based on his experiences on board the vessels during the 1920s. He also remarked that the vermin would not touch the Edam cheeses supplied to the Consolidated Company Ltd. for the feeding of their crews, because they were too hard. In fact, the skipper of the *Exeter* (LT 139) used to cut them up into lumps and, as a joke, bombard the crew with the pieces from the wheelhouse window as they were gutting catches!

Razor-blades: 1. Any of the four types of Razor Shell (*Pharus legumen, Ensis ensis, Ensis siliqua, Solen marginatus*).

Red bait: an irritant substance to the hands found in mackerel guts (specifically, the copepods that constituted part of their diet).

Red herring(s): herrings that were salted in heaps on the ground/floor for two or three days, then smoked for six to eight weeks (or even longer). These were a staple export from Great Yarmouth and Lowestoft to Mediterranean countries for almost 400 years, the trade beginning with shipment to the Italian port of Leghorn (Livorno) during the 1570s. The fish developed a golden/reddish colour from the curing process; hence the name. The metaphorical usage of the term, meaning to divert attention from an issue, may derive in part from Thomas Nashe's pamphlet *Lenten Stuffe* (1599), in which he claimed (among other things) that red herrings were effective in putting hounds off a scent. Nashe's father, William, had been Vicar of Lowestoft from 1561 to 1574 and the young Thomas had lived in the town until he was six years old.

Red herrings and swede: a staple meal among many families during the 1920s and 30s, and one that was both cheap and wholesome. The fish were usually eaten cold (requiring no cooking, because of the length of cure) and the swede boiled, then mashed. "Red herrin' an' swede" became almost a culinary indicator, in Lowestoft, of fishing families at the lower end of the earnings scale.

Red-noses: an alternative term for **lipstick plaice** (q.v.).

Redders: curers specialising in producing red herrings.

Rednecks: a Lowestoft term for Great Yarmouth fishermen. It may have been a reference to the red flannel neckerchiefs worn by some fishermen to prevent chafing by oilskins (even though this practice was not limited to Great Yarmouth) or it may have been a description intended to suggest uncouth behaviour on the part of Yarmouthians. Again, the traditional commercial rivalry between the two towns was responsible for the sobriquet.

Reds: an abbreviated term for **red herrings** (q.v.). In the 1920s and 30s, these were often freely available in some of the Lowestoft pubs (during the winter months) to toast on the bar-room's fire. The thirst generated by eating them generated the need for extra pints of beer to assuage it!

Reef breeze: a sufficiently strong wind to necessitate a vessel's sails being shortened by a single reef.

Reef pennants: the lengths of rope attached to a sail, roven through the *cringles* to enable the sail to be reduced in area (or "reefed") in strong winds.

Reeve: to pass a rope through a hole.

Regatta Day: Lowestoft Regatta, which was held on the last Thursday in August. Lowestoft fishermen liked to be home from the summer herring voyage (to Scotland, followed perhaps by a week or two off the Northumbrian and Yorkshire coasts) in time to enjoy this event. During the late nineteenth century, a sailing contest, or race, between local **smacks** (q.v.) was a notable feature of it. **Yawls** (q.v.) and **Gigs** (q.v.) belonging to local beach companies also competed against each other.

Reining: 1. Strips of old net, which were fastened to the bottom of mackerel nets to act as reinforcing agents. 2. Strips of old net fastened to the bottom of **longshore** (q.v.) drift-nets, which served to weight them down and make them hang better in the water.

Relief money: payments made (usually in the form of food and clothing vouchers) to those people who were out of work and not entitled to unemployment pay.

Relieving officer: a public servant, whose task it was to assess the need of those people applying for poor relief and sanction (or refuse) their application. Junior relieving officers were responsible for issuing the food and clothing vouchers.

Relieving Ta(c)kle: a rope made fast to the tiller-bar of a **smack** (q.v.), which could be led to a block set on the gunwale to either side of it and then used by the helmsman to apply greater leverage on the rudder when steering in heavy weather.

Riddle: 1. To sieve shellfish, in order to eliminate those of inferior size and to get rid of sand and small stones. The word derives from the Old English *hriddel*, meaning "to sift." 2. The term used of a trawl's **tickler** (q.v.) chain stirring up the sediment on the seabed. The image here is a metaphorical one: that of the chain's links acting as a sieve for the sand grains.

Rig: to prepare fishing nets for use. A great deal of expertise went into this, based on knowledge and experience. **Trawls** (q.v.) particularly were subject to a great deal of adjustment, based on the type of ground being worked, the species sought and the skipper's individual requirements.

Rigger: a man who prepared fishing nets for sea and set them up to work effectively.

Ring: 1. A cartel of fish buyers, which acted on the principle of self-interest and sought to exclude outsiders from a market. 2. A bunker-hole in a fishing vessel's deck (the word was mainly used with reference to a trawler's coal-chutes).

Ring-net: a type of seine (usually worked by two boats) used for catching herrings, especially in the Scottish lochs.

Ringing: ring-netting.

Ripper: a hand-line which was worked over the side of a vessel and which had three or four hooks attached to the sinker. It was baited with bits of fish or fish-waste (for demersal species), or had feathers or pieces of silver paper attached (to attract mackerel), and its name derived from the sharp jerk of the hand exercised by the operator when he felt a fish bite. The use of hand-lines, as opportunity afforded, was a means of generating a little extra cash for fishermen or of supplementing their diet on board ship. Apprenticeship agreements of the late sixteenth century make reference to the use of hand-lines on herring and mackerel voyages and stipulated the amount of profit the operator was to have.

Rise: the term used of herrings leaving the seabed and swimming into the upper levels in order to feed.

Riving ma(u)nd: the type of basket used for removing herrings from **vats** (q.v.) and allowing the brine to drain away. The handles were an important part of the construction in performing this task. *Riving maunds* are frequently mentioned in sixteenth and seventeenth century probate inventories relating to people involved in fishing and fish-curing. It is difficult to see any obvious connection with *rive* or *riven*, but it is possible that the baskets were once made from split wands of willow or hazel.

Roads: inshore waters, between the beach and offshore sands, which offered safe anchorage for vessels. The word is an abbreviated form of *roadsteads*, deriving from the Old English *rīdan* meaning, in this case, "to float at anchor" and from *stede* meaning "a place".

Roar: to *rouse* – in this case, meaning to salt herrings down in heaps on the ground, prior to hanging them in the smokehouse. The etymology of the word cannot be precisely established, but it can be found in use as early as 1584, when it occurs in an entry in the Lowestoft manorial records.

Roaring Boys: a nickname given to Pakefield fishermen. This was partly due to association with the process of *roaring* or *rousing* herrings and partly to the reputation they had for being rough and uncouth. There was a story current at one time (it has never been authenticated) that, during the 1820s, the vicar of the parish came upon a group of local men landing a cargo of contraband on the beach. In order that he should not see exactly what was going on, they took hold of him and rammed his head and shoulders into a large rabbit hole at the base of the cliff, making sure that he stayed in that position while they completed their work by hammering a wooden stake between his legs, hard up against his backside. A traditional rhyme goes thus: *The roaring boys of Pakefield, / Oh, nobly they do thrive. / They had but one poor parson / And they buried him alive!*

Roaring-shovel: a wooden shovel, with a slightly hollowed blade, used for salting herrings in heaps on the ground and periodically re-heaping them so as to allow the salt to take effect. This was the first part of the *redding* process.

Rock: an abbreviated form of **rock salmon**.

Rock salmon: dogfish. The euphemism was widely used in the frying trade (it is still current) and applied mainly to the Spur-dog (*Squalus acanthias*) and the Lesser-spotted Dogfish (*Scyliorhinus caniculus*).

Rocket-crew: local volunteers, who manned the rescue equipment described immediately below.

Rocket-line: maritime rescue apparatus developed from the lifesaving mortar invented during the early nineteenth century by Captain W.G. Manby, barrack-master at Great Yarmouth. As used during the twentieth century, the equipment employed rockets to carry a light line from the shore to a wrecked vessel; this would be used to haul a heavier rope to the ship so that the crew could be brought ashore in a breeches buoy.

Roker: specifically, the Thornback Ray (*Raja clavata*), but the term tended to be applied to other rays as well. The word was always pronounced as *rooker* (ruhker). During the summer, the fish were noted as having a distinct smell of ammonia about them, which led to their being used to form the bottom layer in the fish-hold's storage-pounds. The refrigerant qualities of ammonia helped to preserve the ice and thereby improve the quality of the catch. Skate were similarly used, especially in the Irish Sea.

Roker-hook: a gaff used for landing skate and large rays caught on **longlines** (q.v.).

Roky: misty, foggy. The word was always pronounced *rooky* (ruhky). When Macbeth spoke of the crow *making wing to the rooky wood* (Act III, Scene ii), he probably had fog in mind rather than other members of the corvine family.

Roll: the term used of a boat wallowing from side to side in a heavy sea.

Roller: see **Rail roller**.

Roller-gang: a gangway in a vessel's **gunwale** (q.v.) which had an integral roller, to facilitate the free passage of a rope or warp.

Rolls: roes (usually the hard ones – the eggs of the female). The word is a mispronunciation.

Rope: a warp (especially that on a fleet of drift-nets).

Rope-room: the compartment, below decks, on a **drifter** (q.v.) or **smack** (q.v.), in which the warp was coiled (by the cook) as the nets were being hauled, ready for the next shoot. The task was arduous and unpleasant, and it had to be done neatly so as to avoid foul-ups when the gear was next put into operation.

Ropewalk: a part of the North Denes, at Lowestoft, where drifting **warps** (q.v.) were laid out for preservative treatment. It was the same area which had served as a functional ropewalk during the nineteenth century, when ropes were manufactured in the town.

Ross: hard, sandy deposits on the seabed, resembling coral in shape, built up from the casts of polychaetes (marine worms).

Rough-nets: drift-nets made from hemp fibre, which gave them a coarser feel than the later, lighter cotton ones.

Rough-packs: herrings which had been **roused** (q.v.) on the floor of the market, then packed into barrels (sometimes with a layer of ice on top) for export to continental countries – mainly Holland and Belgium.

Rough salt: the coarse-grained salt used for curing herrings. It was usually rock salt mined in Cheshire and brought down by rail.

Rough stuff: 1. A trawlerman's term for the less valuable demersal species, such as whiting and dabs (and even cod, on occasions), as contrasted with **prime fish** (q.v.). 2. A smacksman's term for gurnards and weevers.

Round: a row of meshes on a trawl-net (especially a beam trawl). The term derives from the curve of the net and its generally conical shape.

Rounding: a moderately slender rope, which was wrapped round a wire cable, to form the ground-rope of a trawl.

Rouse: to preserve herrings heaped on the ground, with salt, in the manner described above in **Roar** and **Roaring-shovel**. The word may have originated as a variant of *raise*.

Rove: 1. A tangle of ropes. The term may derive from the name of a textile made from twisted threads of cotton or wool. 2. The head of a copper nail used in fixing the hull's planks to the frame in **clinker-built** (q.v.) boats, or a slightly conical copper washer over which the nail was rivetted or *clenched*. In this particular sense, the word originated from the Old Norse *ró*.

Row: the unit by which the mesh size of drift-nets was reckoned. Thus, 31 rows per yard meant 31 meshes per yard – an average size for the East Anglian autumn voyage. The smaller, summer herrings at North Shields needed nets of 35 or 36 rows per yard, if they were to be caught in viable quantities and not slip from the meshes.

Rows: roes. The pronunciation is not dissimilar.

Rumpy: a Fleetwood term for coral. It may owe something to *rumple*, given the crinkled appearance of some anthozoan colonies.

Run: the term used when a **ring** (q.v.) of fish-buyers pushed the price up at auction, so as to make outsiders pay more than they should have. The term is one used generally of any kind of auction. See also, **Chase**.

Run a trial: to put a new steam fishing-vessel through her trials. These included ascertaining her maximum speed over the **measured mile** (q.v.) and setting her compass.

Run down: to clean drift-nets.

Run for a penny: the term used for the practice whereby young lads in Lowestoft watched out for returning vessels – usually from **The Mount** (q.v.) – and ran to inform crew members' wives that their husbands were in port. They might be rewarded for this service with a penny or halfpenny, or even something to eat (sweets, cakes, or the like).

Run up: 1. To clean drift-nets. 2. To carry news of returning vessels, in the manner described immediately above.

Runner: a Fleetwood term for a **ship's husband** (q.v.) – a term which very much reflects the nature of the job: having to be responsible for all aspects of a vessel's readiness for sea.

Runners: strands of rope or twine.

Running: sailing or steaming with the wind astern.

Running herring: steaming (or rowing, in the case of longshore boats) up and down the length of a fleet of drift-nets and making noise, in the belief that this would cause herrings to rise from the seabed. See also **Banging for herring**.

Runties: Scottish sailing drifters – either **Fifies** (q.v.) or **Zulus** (q.v.). The word may reflect the shorter length (c. 65 feet), broad beam and stout build of these vessels compared with the more elegant, upswept lines of steam drifters.

Rust-tubs: old steam trawlers which had seen better days. The term was used in Lowestoft particularly of the vessels introduced into the town during the 1920s by the Consolidated Fishing Company Ltd. of Grimsby. These craft were no longer viable for trips that necessitated going far from port, but they could be made to pay working the nearer parts of the North Sea. See also, **Crown boats**.

S

Sailed: the word which was always used to describe the ports worked by fishermen, regardless of the type of vessels they served on – whether these were powered by wind, steam or diesel. "We sailed out o' Padstow that year, after soles" or "We sailed out o' Lerwick durin' the summer, most years – after herrins" would have been typical remarks made.

Sailing-and-pulling lifeboat: a lifeboat that was propelled by sails and oars. It was less commonly referred to as a **pulling-and-sailing** (q.v.) vessel.

Sale-ring: a generic term for the place on a fish market where catches were sold. In Lowestoft, it actually was a round building.

Salesman: a fishing company employee who auctioned the catches of his firm's vessels and performed the same task for independent boat-owners. During voyages to other parts of Great Britain, he might also act as **ship's husband** (q.v.) to his company's craft and perform similar duties for independently owned ones.

Salt-water blisters/boils: sores (especially on the neck and wrists) that were caused by the chafing of oilskins on the skin and the action of seawater on those parts affected.

Sample: a **scutcher** (q.v.) of herrings taken at random from the catch and put into a shallow basket, to be sent to the sale-ring for general scrutiny. Catches were sold on the standard of the sample, and there was no point in attempting to conceal a poor-quality catch by carefully selecting the sample because the buyer would either refuse to accept the herrings or drive the agreed price down to a much lower level.

Sample-basket: the basket in which the herring sample was taken to the sale-ring.

Sample-tray: the wooden container in which the sample was displayed at the sale-ring. Each vessel landing had its own individual tray, so potential buyers could make their choice of which catch(es) to purchase.

Sand ray: the Shagreen Ray (*Raja fullonica*).

Sand up: the term used of disturbing the seabed by the **ground-rope** (q.v.) of a trawl, which then caused bottom-dwelling flatfish (like plaice and sole) to rise into the mouth of the approaching net.

San Ditty: the Sandettié Bank, near the Straits of Dover, which was the winter spawning ground for the East Anglian autumn herrings. The East Anglian accent and pronunciation is clear to see (and hear) in this rendering of the location.

Saturday-and-Sunday-night boat: a drifter which did not fish on a Sunday, but which had two nights in port at the weekend. This was usually the result of the owner's (or skipper's) religious convictions and was particularly prevalent among Scottish vessels. In Lowestoft, certain boat-owners who attended **The Bethel** (q.v.) also observed the Sabbath rule.

Sausage-net: a length of net containing spherical glass floats, which was secured to the head-line of a trawl set up to catch hake.

Scabs: fish in poor condition when caught. Sometimes, they would have abrasions of various kinds on the skin.

Scale-money: money deriving from the sale of herring waste for manure and paid, as a Christmas bonus, by some Scotch curers to their men.

Scampi: 1. The Dublin Bay Prawn (*Nephrops norvegicus*). It is fashionable currently to refer to this decapod as *langoustine*. 2. Pieces of flesh from the tail end of the Angler Fish (*Lophius piscatorius*), which were often used as a passable scampi substitute. See also **Monkfish**.

Scandalise: to reduce a sail's area by lowering the gaff. The term was used particularly in association with a steam drifter's mizzen sail. It derives from *scantle*, meaning "to reduce" or "make small".

Scolter: a dolphin. Sometimes the term was used with reference to the Porpoise (*Phocæna communis*).

Scooped out: a term used to describe a fishing ground which had been cleaned out by excessive trawling.

Score: a steep alleyway or flight of steps (and sometimes the two combined) linking the top of a cliff with the base. Lowestoft has eleven of these altogether, serving as roadways or foot tracks. They were originally surface-water drainage channels on the face of the cliff, which became used by people as ways up and down. The word derives from the Old Norse *skora*, meaning "to make an incision".

Scores: rows of twenty cod at a time, laid out on the floor of the Lowestoft fish market for display and sale. This was the way that cod were auctioned up to the time of the First World War.

Scotch boiler: the standard type of boiler, on steam engines, in which the fire-tubes are surrounded by water. The first element of the term may reflect the pioneering use of steam-propulsion in Scottish fishing vessels during the last quarter of the nineteenth century.

Scotch cure: the method of pickling herrings by removing the gills and long gut, then packing the fish "sardine-fashion" in a barrel. Each layer of fish was sprinkled with salt and was placed at a right-angle to the one below. This method of cure was not peculiarly Scottish, but was refined in that country during the second half of the nineteenth century. The Dutch had been masters of the method during the sixteenth and seventeenth centuries, but it can be traced back to southern Sweden in the late thirteenth century.

Scotch girl: a woman of any age, from thirteen or fourteen to her sixties, who gutted, sized and packed herrings for the pickling process.

Scotch nets: herring nets that were made from cotton. This fibre began to take over from hemp during the nineteenth century because it was both lighter and more effective at enmeshing herrings. In 1820, James Paterson established a factory at Musselburgh for producing cotton nets on power looms and the process was further improved in 1835 when Walter Ritchie, of Leith, developed a mechanical means of tightening the knots. From this point, the cotton net was produced in ever-increasing numbers and the amount of fish caught increased accordingly.

Scotch voyage: the summer voyage to Shetland and the east coast of Scotland, to catch herrings.

Scran: inferior and discarded herrings, left lying around on a fish market. The term is probably a derivative of *scrannel*, meaning "thin" or "meagre", and this word itself may be compared with the Norwegian *skran*, meaning "shrivelled".

Scranners: fish market scavengers, who made a bare living from what they picked up and sold on.

Scratchers: a Milford Haven/Fleetwood term for the East Anglian drifter-trawlers, which visited those ports for trawling voyages in the Irish Sea during the late spring and summer. The specific reference is to these vessels' comparatively light **otter gear** (q.v.) merely "scratching" the seabed, in comparison with the heavier west-side trawls used by vessels from the Welsh and Lancashire ports.

Screw: a steam or diesel craft's propeller.

Screwing up: the term used to describe the process of trying to get a steam or diesel vessel into position, in order to land its catch. Unless the herring market at Lowestoft was unusually quiet, it was not possible to lie broadside on to the quay and the boats had to access what space there was head on. Skippers would therefore squeeze their way in on the engine, between the vessels lying on either side, using what power was required to achieve their goal. *Screwing up*, therefore, refers both to the use of the propeller (or *screw*) and to the boring action required to access the quay. If a lot of vessels were seeking to land at the same time, it was not unusual to hear the cracking of timbers on wooden craft, and tempers became frayed. One of the **berthing masters** (q.v.) at Lowestoft, noted for his ready turn of phrase, was heard one day (during the 1930s) to issue the following order: "Boy Roy, stop stickin' your snout up the Girl Gladys's arse!" Both names referred to wooden steam-drifters belonging to the same owner, J.V. Breach – their registration numbers being LT 1167 and LT 1174, respectively.

Scrogs: continental fishermen (especially the Dutch). The word may be a variant of *scrags*.

Scruff ground: a term used of fishing grounds with a rough, shelly bottom. The first element can be traced back to the sixteenth century as meaning "litter" or "refuse" and may itself have derived from *scurf*.

Scud: to shake herrings (or sprats) from the meshes of a **drift-net** (q.v.). It is difficult to see any connection with other meanings of the word, unless the quick, coordinated shaking of the nets derived from the use of *scud* meaning "hurried movement

Scudding-pole: a round spar set above the edge of the hold, against which fishermen braced themselves when hauling drift-nets.

Scuffle: the term used of the wind causing movement on the surface of the sea. The sense of disturbance is not hard to visualise and the word may well derive from the Swedish *skuff(a)*, meaning "to push".

Scuffly: a term used to describe choppy water.

Scummers/skummers: herrings which fell from the meshes as the nets came inboard and were caught in a **didall** (q.v.). This task was usually performed by the **driver** (q.v.) and the fish he salvaged were usually his to sell. The term may well have derived from *skim*.

Scuppit: a wooden shovel, with a slightly hollowed blade. The word may have derived from *scoop*.

Scutcher: a metal or wooden scoop (usually the former) used in the hold to put herrings into quarter-cran baskets, prior to them being run ashore. The artefact was not unlike an elongated dustpan and, in view of this shape, the word probably derives from the Latin *scutum*, meaning "a shield".

Scuttles: the scuppers. The term is a simple mispronunciation. Given the function of the scuppers in clearing water from a vessel's decks, the word *scupper* itself may derive from the post-classical Latin *skuppire*, meaning "to spit".

Sea-salts: herrings which were salted down on board a drifter, awaiting its return to port.

Sea-sticking: the initial filling and stacking of Scotch-cure barrels (upright and three tiers high).

Sea trout: a form of the native Trout (*Salmo trutta*) – sometimes referred to as the Brown Trout – which spends part of its life in the sea. Its migration(s), spawning habits and general development are similar to those of the Salmon (*Salmo salar*).

Seaweed rash: an alternative term for **curly weed rash** (q.v.).

Second hand: a term used in some British fishing-ports at one time for the **mate** (q.v.) on board a vessel. The thinking behind the expression, clearly, is that the master or skipper was the "first hand".

Secondhand buying: the purchase of fish which had already been bought by someone else at a lower price. This was sometimes done by fish merchants to make up shortfalls in their supplies or to make sure that favoured customers got the fish they needed.

Seconds: damaged or inferior smoked herrings – especially **kippers** (q.v.).

Seed herring: small, immature herrings – a term broadly comparable with **whitebait** (q.v.).

Seine(-net): any kind of movable net, designed to hang in the water and form a bag (in which to enclose the catch) when the ends are drawn together. In Lowestoft, the term usually referred to the **Danish Seine** (q.v.), a method of stationary trawling adopted during the 1920 and 30s for catching haddock on the Dogger Bank.

Seize: to whip, or lash, the end of a rope with twine.

Seizing: a length of rope on a **drift**-net (q.v.), which joined the back-rope to the warp. It was twenty-four feet long and made of four strands. This sense of the word, meaning "attaching" or binding" can be traced back to the middle of the seventeenth century.

Selecting: sorting gutted herrings into one or other of the sizes required (there were seven in all) for the **Crown Brand** (q.v.) category of pickles. The women did this as they gutted and were very accurate with regard to the length(s) specified.

Selections: the different sizes of herring laid down for Scotch cure (especially those pickles which carried the Crown Brand mark).

Set: 1. To take up a position for shooting drift-nets. 2. To sit. This mispronunciation is common in East Anglia, either by default or because it is a dialect survival from an earlier period of history.

Set-net: a bag net, fixed to a square wooden frame and set in mid-water (anchored to the seabed and floated up on top), to catch fish on the principle of tidal flow.

Set-pole: a long wooden **quant** (q.v.), with a forked end, which was used at launchings to push yawls and lifeboats through the breakers into deeper water.

Settling: 1.The pay-off for crew members at the end of a fishing voyage. 2. The term used for the shrinking of the tiers of herrings in Scotch cure barrels. After ten days had elapsed from the initial packing, the barrels were topped up with **blood pickle** (q.v.) and fish of identical age.

Shale: a tapering wooden rod, which was used to check the dimensions of fishing net meshes.

Shank: 1. The length of a fish hook between the eye and the bowl (curve).

The analogy with the human *tibia* is an obvious one and the word connects linguistically with the Old English *scéanca* and the Middle Low German *schenke*. 2. An individual length of **longline** (q.v.). A number of these were tied together to make up the whole line.

Shannocking: longlining for cod in the North Sea from drifters or drifter-trawlers. To *shannock* was a Norfolk dialect word meaning to go longshore fishing (off the northern coast of the county). It was also the term used for an inhabitant of the town of Sheringham, many of whom were involved in fishing close to land. Because the Lowestoft vessels did much of their longlining on sandbanks lying to the north-east of the Norfolk coast, where Sheringham and its neighbour, Cromer, were situated, the term here may well be an example of adoption by location. Some people believe that the origin of shannock is to be found in the old dialect word *shanny*, meaning "high-spirited" or "scatter-brained".

Share system: the method of structuring a drifter's finances with regard to expenses and profits. There is not sufficient space to go into detail here, but the vessel owner's proportion of the money taken in Great Yarmouth gave fishermen better remuneration than it did in Lowestoft. The best paid crew member was the skipper (at one and a quarter shares, perhaps even one and a half) and the lowest was the cook (a half-share). However, the system was flexible and variations of the basic allotments were often found.

Share fisherman: see no. 1 immediately below.

Shareman: 1. Any fisherman paid on the principle of a stipulated share of a vessel's net earnings. It related particularly to men involved in herring-catching. 2. The member of a steam drifter's crew who was paid a full share – i.e. the **hawseman** (q.v.).

Sheep: white cumulus clouds (especially those seen in summer).

Sheer: 1. The word used to describe very clear seawater. The derivation here is from the Middle English *shire*, meaning "clear" or "pure". 2. To steer, or turn, to port or starboard. The element of control from the helm inherent in the term can be traced back to the early eighteenth century. 3. The upward sweep of a vessel's deck towards the bow. The image here is one of steepness and the term has been in use since the 1690s.

Sheer-legs: a large three-legged crane, with the legs bolted together at the upper extremity, which was erected on a quayside and used for raising and lowering heavy machinery. One stood on the north side of the inner harbour at Lowestoft and was much in demand for the fitting of engines and boilers, and for removing these when occasion demanded; there was a similar one at Southtown, Great Yarmouth.

Sheet: the rope attached to the lower, after corner of a sail and used to extend the sail or alter its set.

Shelf: to store demersal fish (especially cod) in the hold of a trawler by laying them belly down on a layer of crushed ice, which had first been spread on boards placed in the pounds.

Shetland: the generic term used for the summer herring voyage to the Shetland Isles and the east coast of Scotland.

Shetland boots: leather sea-boots which reached to mid-calf. These were worn on the summer herring voyage to Scotland and were a lighter boot for the conditions than the thigh-length ones worn during the autumn and winter.

Shields boat: a steam drifter which did not go any further north in the search for herrings than North Shields. Vessels of this kind tended to be the smaller, older ones built at the end of the nineteenth century and the beginning of the twentieth.

Shields herring: the herrings which were caught off North Shields during the late summer. These were smaller than the East Anglian autumn stock, with a high fat content and a tendency to burst if not carefully handled. They made excellent kippers.

Shiftenings: changes of underclothes which fishermen took away with them on a voyage. Forby records the word (albeit in a different context) in *The Vocabulary of East Anglia*. The derivation of the term is from *shift*, meaning "to change".

Shilling mesh: a drift-net of 35/36 **rows** (q.v.) per yard. This type of gear was used to catch the smaller herrings off North Shields (as referred to above) and got its name from each mesh being approximately similar in size to a shilling coin. The term also served to differentiate this type of net from ones of the usual size at 31 rows per yard.

Shimmer: a quantity of herrings taken in a single haul. The amount is unspecified, being neither large nor small, but it represented a satisfactory quantity of fish. The term is obviously metaphorical and has a certain degree of attractiveness about it. It probably derives from the Old English *scýmrian* or the Middle Dutch *schēmeren*, meaning "to glimmer" or "to glitter".

Ship a sea: the term used of a vessel having the waves strike it broadside on and swamp the decks.

Ship in: to join a drifter or trawler as a crew member.

Ship up: to provide a vessel with crew members – a duty that was usually the responsibility of the **ship's husband** (q.v.).

Shipped up: to be given a job on a fishing vessel. Thus, a man might say, "I got shipped up on the *Hosanna*."

Ship's husband: a shore-worker who was responsible for crewing a vessel and making sure that it was ready for sea. Taking note of the fact that fishing craft were always given female gender, the analogy here is obvious. A ship's husband was usually a man who had had some years' previous experience of fishing.

Shirt-bag: a canvas bag, with a draw string, in which spare changes of clothes were carried. Fishermen took shirt-bags away with them on the major voyages.

Shoals (The): a group of sandbanks situated to the north-east of the Norfolk coast, which include the Leman, the Ower and the Swarte. The word *shoal* derives from the Old English *sćeald*, meaning "shallow". Middle English gave it the meaning of "sandbank", because of the lesser depth of water above such a feature.

Shod: a beachmen's wooden shed, usually situated somewhere near the shoreline. This may have been a particular beach company's headquarters or a smaller building used for the storage of equipment. The pronunciation here is met with in parts of East Anglia other than those along the coast.

Shoe-kettle: a metal, lidded, cooking utensil, shaped like a boot or shoe, which was used on board sailing smacks. It was designed for insertion into a boiler's furnace (in this case, the one belonging to the capstan) and could be left safely for long periods of time. It was sometimes referred to simply as "the shoe" and it was customarily left partially in the boiler-fire to keep tea permanently on the brew.

Shoot: 1. To cast fishing nets or lines. 2. To swim quickly (a term used of fish and customarily applied to mackerel).

Shooting-in stuff: lengths of net used to mend split trawls.

Shooting-roller: a wooden roller fixed along the side of a drifter's hold, to facilitate the pulling up of the nets during shooting.

Shooting-stick: a wooden rod used to flick **longlines** (q.v.) over the side of the vessel. It greatly reduced the danger of getting a hook caught in the hand.

Shoreman: a man who helped to launch a lifeboat or yawl, but who wasn't actually a crew member.

Short Blues: vessels belonging to the Hewett family's fleet of smacks, which moved from Barking and based themselves at Gorleston in 1854. There were eighty of these altogether at one time (during the 1880s) and they got their name from the company's small, square, blue flag which every vessel flew at its mainmast head. A public house called *The Short Blue* is still in business on Gorleston High Street.

Short sea(s): a term used, largely of the North Sea, to describe the type of waves encountered. Put simply, the length of *fetch* (i.e. the distance over which wind and tide combine to produce the size of waves) was far less in the southern North Sea than in the Atlantic Ocean. This, in turn, led to smaller, choppier waves than the Atlantic *rollers* – conditions which sometimes led to greater discomfort on board ship.

Shot: a catch of fish taken in a single haul. The term was especially applied to herrings.

Shot(ten): a term used of fish that had spawned. It usually referred to herrings and can be traced back to the mid-fifteenth century. The word is an old form of the past participle of the verb "shoot" and effectively means "discharged" – the reference being, in this case, to the fish's roes.

Show the broom: a practice adopted by some Dutch fishermen in the North Sea, to show their superiority over the English. A deck broom would be picked up and waved at passing ships. This was a direct reference back to the third quarter of the seventeenth century when the Dutch admiral, Cornelis Tromp, had boasted that he would sweep the English battle-fleet from the seas and had ordered the hoisting of a broom at the beginning of any engagement with enemy vessels.

Shreave: a sheave (i.e. a grooved wheel set in a wooden block, which allowed a rope to run freely). The term is a simple mispronunciation.

Shrimper: a generic term for a single-masted, gaff-rigged **longshore boat** (q.v.) of the kind used at Great Yarmouth and Lowestoft. Shrimps formed only part of such vessels' catches. At other times, they would fish for demersal species and also for herrings and sprats.

Shruff: wood shavings – especially from oak, which was valued as the fuel for smokehouse fires. The term probably derives from the German *schroff*, meaning "a fragment of mineral or metal".

Side-cords: the double length of twine at the top and bottom of a **drift-net** (q.v.), which served to reinforce the meshes.

Side-winder: a diesel trawler which shot and hauled its gear from the side (usually the starboard). This was the common method until *stern-trawlers* were increasingly developed during the 1960s and 70s. These particular craft worked their gear over a specially constructed and lowered stern. The diesel vessel *Mincarlo* (LT 412), which was built in 1962, is a good example of a *side-trawler* and is undergoing progressive restoration. She is run by the same independent charitable trust as the ***Lydia Eva*** (q.v.) and may be visited at the Heritage Quay, Lowestoft, from May to October.

Sides: the top and bottom of a drift-net.

Sign on: to register at a labour exchange, when out of work, so as to be able to draw unemployment pay. Trawlermen were able to do this, as wage-earners. Driftermen could not, because they were classified as self-employed.

Silver eel: the Common Eel (*Anguilla anguilla*), at that stage of its life-cycle when it migrates to the Atlantic Ocean, prior to spawning in the Sargasso Sea. The skin on the belly of the fish becomes shiny and silvery.

Silver herrings: see **Soft-cure** below.

Single knot: the knot that secured the tie around a drift-net at the end of a voyage and indicated that it was only slightly damaged. It was otherwise known as a **figure-eight** (q.v.) knot because of its appearance and was formed by simply crossing the ends of the tie and pulling them through.

Sinkers: dumplings which had not risen while being cooked and were therefore of a sticky and heavy texture.

Sit like duck: an evocative description of a sailing smack under way in a stiff breeze, with her mainsail reefed, her hull slightly heeled over, and with everything under control. The image is one of ease and stability.

Skate: a generic term used in the frying trade for rays of all kinds. In fish and chip shops today, there is a more than even chance of "skate" being **roker** (q.v.).

Skeet: see **Skid**.

Skeleton-ropes: ground-ropes on trawls which had no **dangles** (q.v.) or chains attached.

Skid: a wooden bar, four to five feet long, with a strip of greased metal fixed to the top, which was used for moving longshore boats across a beach. A series of these would be placed under the keel and the vessel pushed or pulled across them. The term is local, Lowestoft variant of **skeet**.

Skillen/Skillen Corner: the fishing grounds near Terschelling Island, off the north-west coast of Holland. The mispronunciation derives from the second element of "Terschelling".

Skinner's Knoll (The): the corner close to the Lowestoft **trawl dock** (q.v.), at the turning of Waveney Road into London Road North. It was given this nickname because, during the 1920s and 30s, unemployed fishermen (especially skippers and mates) used to congregate there in the hope of meeting up with an acquaintance who had just landed a catch and "skinning" a drink from him in either the *The Bank Stores* or *The Anchor* – public houses located not far away in Commercial Road.

Skipper-owner: a fisherman who owned and commanded his own vessel (usually a drifter or drifter-trawler). The word *skipper* itself probably derives from the Middle Low German or Middle Dutch *schipper*, meaning "someone who owns a ship".

Skipper-rows: two residential streets at the north end of Lowestoft (Sussex Road and Worthing Road) which were developed during the Edwardian period, when the fishing industry was at its most profitable. A number of local skippers were able to afford the purchase price of the smart, new, terraced "villas" and their concentration in this area led to the name. It was considered the height of fashion and good taste at the time to have a piano standing in the front room (even though no one in the house was able to play it!) and a potted aspidistra in the bay window.

Skipper's log: a record kept by individual masters of their fishing activities, year on year, as an attempted means of maximising a vessel's earnings. See also, **Log book**.

Skylight: the overhead window in the **casing** (q.v.) of a fishing vessel's engine-room, which was usually divided into four separate panes. Each of these opened on a sliding arm, in order to provide ventilation.

Slab: a plaice which had recently spawned and had not begun to fatten up. The quality of the flesh was poor, both in terms of texture and flavour, and the term is more likely to reflect its watery nature than the actual shape of the fish. *Slabby* is a sixteenth-century dialect word for anything wet or slushy.

Slack away: to unhitch the **tissot** (q.v.) on a fleet of drift-nets and let more warp out, before making fast again.

Slack water: the point before the turn of the tide to ebb or flow. Hence, there is a *low-water slack* and a *high-water slack*.

Sleeping: spawning (the term was used exclusively of herrings).

Slice: a long steel rod, with a flattened and broadened end, pierced through rather in the manner of the kitchen implement, which was used for loosening coal and clinker in steam-engine furnaces.

Slink: a mature cod which had little flesh on it relative to its overall size. The word may be suggestive of an aborted or prematurely born (and, therefore, less than perfectly formed) calf or other farm animal, because *slink* had this particular meaning at one time. By the end of the seventeenth century, it had become used as a term for anything lank or lean.

Slip: 1. A half-grown sole. This metaphorical usage is first recorded in 1881 and probably has its origins in the idea of a cutting being taken from a parent stock to create a new plant. 2. The sliding wooden shutters on a bunk in a fishing vessel's cabin.

Slop: a loose-fitting, calico garment, reaching to below the waist, which was often worn by fishermen in fine weather. The word dates back to the medieval period.

Slushy: a term used to describe vessels which had a tendency to roll and therefore ship water. Such craft were usually broad-beamed, of comparatively shallow draught and with a not particularly well-defined keel.

Smack: 1. A generic term for any kind of fishing vessel (above the size of longshore craft) which was powered by sail. 2. A gaff-rigged sailing trawler. The *Excelsior* (LT 472), built in 1921, at the local John Chambers yard, Oulton Broad, is the last working Lowestoft smack left. She is managed by an independent charitable trust and is able to perform a number of maritime functions. A typical Lowestoft vessel of the late nineteenth/early twentieth century was c. 70 feet long, by 18-19 feet in the beam, and with a hold depth of 9 feet.

Smacking: trawling, on a smack. Thus, a man might say, "I went smackin' that year in the *Rose o' Devon*."

Smack paintings: ship portraits of sailing trawlers, which were produced for vessel-owners and crew members (mainly skippers). See also, **Pierhead paintings**.

Smacksman: a fisherman who worked on board a **smack** (q.v.). The term is remembered in the eponymously-named folksong, *The Smacksman* (see Appendix 2).

Small boat: a drifter's or trawler's lifeboat. The term is identical with **little boat** (q.v.).

Smash: to have a try at fishing any kind of ground, as time and opportunity afforded. Thus, a skipper might say, "We wuz down orf the Brown Ridges, an' that wuz a beau'iful night, so I thought we'd have a smash." The term tended to be applied to trawling rather than to drifting.

Smash-and-grab gear: bridle trawl-gear., without **quarter-ropes** (q.v.), used for quick shooting and hauling in Arctic waters.

Smokehouse: a building of varying size (depending on the scale of the enterprise) in which herrings were hung to cure above slow-burning sawdust fires. Vents or louvers in the roof-ridge, or the upper part of the walls, allowed a current of air to circulate and the smoke to escape. Brick was the customary material used to construct smokehouses, but wooden ones were not unknown.

Smoker: a smoking concert. The word was always pronounced *smooker* (smuhker).

Smoking concert: an annual entertainment which was held in a beach company's headquarters. It was for men only.

Snag: the term used of a trawl net catching on rough ground and the meshes getting torn. The word may well have its origin in the Norwegian *snage*, meaning "sharp point" or "spike".

Snood: a piece of twine which secured a hook to a longline. Snoods were of varying length, according to the kind of fishing being carried out. The usage is first recorded in 1682.

Snotch: to make diagonal incisions along the backs of fresh herrings, prior to frying them. This made it easier to lift the flesh from the backbone. The word itself is a variant of *notch*.

Snout: the bow(s) of a vessel. The analogy with the position and shape of the human nose is easily understood. See also, **Screwing up**.

Snud: a snood. The word is an example of variant pronunciation.

Soft-cure: herrings that were lightly salted and smoked, as opposed to the *hard cure* which produced red herrings. Soft-cure herrings were not much produced during the later years of the industry, but had been popular at one time for export to Mediterranean countries. The fish were

At the **smokehouse**, herring on a **speet** as this traditional method of preserving the fish gets under way. These could be **bloaters** or **red herrings**; gutted and split before smoking would make them **kippers**.

salted down on the ground for a day or so, then hung in the smokehouse for a week to ten days. They were sometimes referred to as *silver herrings*. A slightly longer period of cure would produce **goldens** (q.v.).

Solan birds/geese/gulls: Gannets (*Sula bassana*). The word derives from the Old Norse *súla*, which can be seen retained in the species' Latin classification name. The presence of these birds was a good indicator of shoals of fish.

Sole-plate: the **bed-plate** (q.v.) of a marine steam-engine.

Sole-tub: a shallow wooden tub in which soles were washed after they had been gutted. Soles, as a high-value fish, were given careful treatment.

Sowle: Southwold. This is an old, variant name for the Suffolk town. Another form is to be seen in "Sole Bay", the name given to that area of the North Sea offshore from the town. An ancient slander, directed at the inhabitants of nearby Walberswick, goes thus: "He's a Walserwig whisperer. You can hear him over in Sowle!"

Sparky: an employee of the Marconi company who operated radio transmitting and receiving sets on board non-Naval shipping. This function was mainly associated with the Merchant Marine, but a number of the larger steam trawlers (particularly those based in distant-water ports) had "sparkies" as part of the crew during the 1920s and 30s – a practice that continued during the diesel era after the Second World War. In addition to their weekly wage (paid by Marconi), these operatives were also awarded an *ex gratia* payment of about £1 per £100 of **gross earnings** (q.v.). Messages were received and sent in morse code.

Spars: 1. Wooden net-drying posts and frames, which stood on the North Denes at Lowestoft, some of which can still be seen in that part retained as a conservation area. They are not unlike football goals, but lower, with thicker uprights and a more slender horizontal member. 2. The horizontal wooden bars, which were fixed to masts and carried sails.

Speet: a wooden rod onto which herrings were threaded, through mouth and gill-case, prior to being hung in the smokehouse (bloaters and red herrings were given this treatment). Sprats were also *speeted* prior to being smoked, but on much narrower rods. The word is a variant of *spit*.

Spell: a break from hauling on board a fishing vessel. This usually occurred during difficult weather conditions.

Spell-buffs: painted floats which marked the quarter, half, three-quarter and final stages of a fleet of drift-nets. When a spell-buff came inboard, the men hauling the nets would often change position with each other, both for variety and relief – the middle of the net always reckoned to be the hardest part of the work, when **scudding** (q.v.).

Spell round: to change position (and duties, if going from lint to buffs) when hauling drift-nets. The first instance of *spell*, used in the sense of switching-round, is recorded in 1593.

Spents: herrings which had spawned and had not yet begun to recover. See **Shotten**, above.

Spike (the): the workhouse – a slang-term, originally, of the mid-nineteenth century, deriving from the "sharpness" of the treatment of inmates. See also, **Test work**.

Spile: a small, tapering, wooden plug in the top end of a Scotch cure barrel, which allowed venting to take place, if required. The word derives from the Middle Low German and Middle Dutch *spile* and may be compared with the North Frisian *spīl*.

Spinnaker: the largest of all the **jibs** (q.v.) used on smacks. It was a sail used to give a vessel greater way in calm weather conditions. The word is said to derive from *Sphinx*, the first yacht to carry such a sail (in 1866), but it may also owe something to *spanker* – a gaff-rigged sail set on a boom at the aftermost part of a vessel.

Splice: to join two lengths of rope by unravelling and re-plaiting the individual strands. The origin of the word is probably the Middle Dutch *splissen*.

Split: 1. To gut herrings and split them along the backbone as the first part of the kippering process. 2. A damaged drift-net, particularly one where the meshes had been torn by Spur-dogs (*Squalus acanthias*).

Split-arses: dumplings which had cracked open during the cooking process. The comparison with human buttocks requires no comment!

Spoilts: drift-nets which had been torn or damaged in some way.

Spotty: the term used of unpredictable catches of fish, especially herrings.

Sprag: 1. A half-grown cod. The term is first recorded in 1875, having been applied to young salmon almost a century earlier. 2. To bar someone from an activity of some kind or deny them access to a particular place.

Spragged: 1. Arrested (and fined) for illegal fishing. 2. Banned from fishing because of illicit activity.

Spratting: the term applied to the late autumn inshore fishery for sprats. The species (*Sprattus sprattus*) was an important source of income for local

longshoremen (q.v.) and the season usually lasted from early November up till about Christmas.

Spring herring(s): recovering **spents** (q.v.), which were caught off the East Anglian coast during April.

Springing: fishing for spring herrings. This was a voyage of very limited length and involved only a few vessels (usually, older drifters), but it filled a gap in the market and could therefore be profitable.

Sprinkle: to shake salt (from a hand-held, shallow metal dish) onto herrings, as they were put into **klondyke boxes** (q.v.)

Spronk/sprunk: the term used for one strand of a drift-net's mesh being broken. The term may derive from *sprung* which, as the past participle of "spring", had the meaning of *split* attached to it at the end of the sixteenth century.

Spunyarn: rope yarns which were twisted together to make a line for general use in rigging. It was especially useful for making *shrouds*. The term can be traced back to the third decade of the seventeenth century.

Square: the top part of a trawl net, between the head-line and the **batings** (q.v.).

Square off: to make a vessel tidy and put everything in order at the end of a voyage.

Square up: 1. To **square off**, as immediately above. 2. To line up a beam trawl at right-angles to a smack's stern, before releasing the gear to the seabed.

Squibs: squid – usually the Common Squid (*Loligo forbesi*). The name is a simple mispronunciation.

Srad: the Allis Shad (*Alosa alosa*). This is a strange mispronunciation, but one that was not uncommon among previous generations of fishermen.

Stages: the wooden piers at Lerwick, at which herrings were landed during the summer fishing season.

Stanchions: vertical supports in the hull of a boat, which were often used as partition posts in the fish-hold. The word derives from the Old French *estanchon*, meaning "a prop" or "support".

Standard boat: a drifter (86-88 feet long) built to Admiralty specifications during World War I. Steam fishing vessels of all kinds were requisitioned in large numbers for patrolling and minesweeping duties, and so effective did they prove that the Admiralty commissioned a standard version of its own. The Lowestoft firm of John Chambers was lead yard for the building of wooden *standard drifters*. At the cessation of hostilities, many of these vessels were sold off into private ownership and equipped for fishing. *Standard trawlers*, built of steel, were also constructed during the wartime period in various British shipyards.

Stapling: a length of tarred twine which was used on a **beam trawl** (q.v.) to secure the net to the bolch line, along the lower wings and bosom.

Staysail: a triangular sail which was occasionally rigged on the fore-side of a sailing vessel's mizzen.

Steaming: the term used of a vessel travelling on the outward or homeward leg of a fishing voyage. It also applied to the journey to and from fishing grounds being worked at any one time. The change from steam to diesel engines saw it continue in use, and it is still being used today.

The drifter *Shepherd Lad* **steaming** out of Lowestoft harbour about 1960. On her foredeck is the **capstan**; the **mainmast** or **foremast** is laid back and the skipper steers from the **wheelhouse**.

Steer off: the term used for a crew member taking over the wheel of a vessel after the skipper or mate had negotiated the harbour on the outward run.

Stem: 1. The bow of a vessel. 2. The vertical post at the bow, erected on the keel and one of the main parts of a vessel's frame. Variant roots of this word are to be found in a number of the ancient North European languages (Old English, Old Frisian and Old Norse among them) and, up to the end of the medieval period, it referred to the vertical timber at either end of a vessel. By the middle of the sixteenth century, it had come to mean the prow, or the bows.

Stem-end: a term used of a fleet of drift-nets, to indicate the nets and ropes nearest to the drifter itself.

Stem-end net: the last drift-net shot and therefore the one closest to the vessel.

Stem-post: the bow post of a vessel,

Stem the tide: to sail or steam against the tide.

Stepping: step-dancing of a traditional kind, in which the dancer (usually, but not exclusively, male) kept to one spot and varied movement of the legs and feet in time with the music. It was a popular pastime among some fisherman, especially those from coastal villages, and light-footedness was an admired quality. The writer was once told, "There wuz this gret big ol' boy out at Kessingland an' he could step on a plate without breakin' it!"

Stern-dragger: a *stern-trawler*.

Stern-tube: the "tunnel" in the after-end of a steam vessel, through which the propeller shaft passed. In drifters, it was made of *lignum vitae* splines, this particular Caribbean hardwood (*Guaiacum officinale* or *Guaiacum sanctum*) being resistant both to the rotting effect of seawater and the friction caused by the rotation of the shaft.

Sticky-bag: a canvas *poke* lined with tallow, which was reputedly used during the late nineteenth century to cheat innumerate herring fishermen. The boat-owner would put out a man's earnings on a table in front of him (in sovereigns and coins of smaller denomination), then rake the money back into the bag, before shooting it out again onto the table. Some of the coins would be retained by the tallow and the fisherman, not being able to count, would not know he had been cheated.

Stiff alive: the term used to describe trawlfish landed in first-class condition. It applied more to the catches of **smacks** (q.v.) than of steam trawlers, as the former vessels covered the ground more slowly than the latter and beam trawls were a "gentler" form of fishing than **otter gear** (q.v.).

Stiff build: a term used of the hull-structure of a sailing smack, to depict its rigidity and strength. Lowestoft smacksmen always reckoned that vessels built in Rye were the most robust craft, with those emanating from Brixham of more "elastic" construction.

Stir: a slight, visible disturbance on the surface of the sea, resulting from the wind, in fine weather conditions.

Stock-boats: coasters which brought **farlanes** (q.v.) and pickle barrels down to East Anglia from Scotland for the autumn herring voyage.

Stock herring: large, prime, East Anglian autumn herrings, which would suit any kind of curing treatment and were especially valued by the Dutch and Belgians when **vatted** (q.v.). One of the advantages of the local herrings was the relatively low fat content of the fish, which made it much less perishable (about 7% of total weight, as opposed to as much as 20-25% in the summer herrings caught at Shetland or North Shields).

Stocker-bait: 1. A trawlerman's share of the money made from the sale of lesser species, such as weevers (specifically, the Greater Weever – *Trachinus draco*) and gurnards. This was a standard way of supplementing wages. 2. A drifterman's share of the money made from the sale of net cleanings and species taken incidentally to herrings and mackerel. There is no accepted explanation of the origin of the term, but it may derive from the expression "stock of bait", which would soon become "stock o' bait" in everyday pronunciation. The odds and ends of fish allowed crew members as a perquisite were the type of thing which would have been used at one time to bait handlines.

Stockholm tar: a type of pitch used for tarring warps and sealing buffs. Some fishermen also recommended it as a remedy for piles – probably working on the principle that the discomfort caused by applying it would outweigh that caused by the haemorrhoids themselves. The following comment was once made by a **ransacker** (q.v.) of the author's acquaintance: "Stockholm tar – the finest thing there is for piles. You shove that up yuh backside, an' you dun't worry about piles no more!"

Stockie: an abbreviated form of **stocker-bait**.

Stoker: the second engineer on a drifter or trawler. An important part of his duties was attending to the furnace.

Stone-trap: a crescent-shaped slit (about three feet long) in the underpart of a trawl-net's cod-end, below the **flopper** (q.v.), through which stones and rocks could pass and thereby prevent damage to the net.

Stones: sizeable pieces of rock (small boulders even) which were trawled up in certain areas of the North Sea , before the **flapper** (q.v.) became widely adopted. It was often the practice of skippers to keep them on board for a while, before jettisoning them in locations where no particular amount of trawling took place. H. Harvey George, manager of the Hewett **Short Blue** (q.v.) fleet of smacks in Gorleston during the later nineteenth century, gave specific orders to the company's skippers to bring all such material home from the Dogger Bank. It was then used to make the terracing in the steeply sloping garden of his house (*The Towers*) on Gorleston High Street and can still be seen *in situ* today.

Stopper: 1. A plaited length of rope, of lesser breaking strain than a beam trawl's warp, which was wrapped round the latter and attached to the towing post. If the gear came fast, the stopper would break rather than the more expensive warp. 2. A **seizing** (q.v.). 3. A length of wire cable between trawl net and otter doors (see also, **Legs**). The use of *stopper*, meaning "a piece of rope to secure something", is first met with in the 1620s.

Store: a commonly used abbreviated form of **net-store** (q.v.).

Storm-jib: a small triangular sail set on mainmast stay and bowsprit, to help keep a smack steady in bad weather. It was the smallest of all the jibs carried.

Stow up: 1. To tidy up fishing nets ready for the next shoot. 2. To pack nets away, ready for a return to port.

Stranded: the term used to describe a rope with one or more strands broken.

Strike: the term used of pelagic fish (herrings, mackerel, pilchards and sprats) making contact with the meshes of drift-nets.

String: a beachman's slang term for the first securing rope used in a salvage operation. Whoever was first to get a rope onto a stricken vessel had the legal right to claim salvage. This ancient custom might well be described thus: "That allus used t' be a bit of a race, t' see who could git a string aboard fust."

Strop: 1. A length of rope on a **drift-net** (q.v.) joining the head-rope, or cork-line, to the buff. It was either fifteen or eighteen feet long and made of three strands. Strops were of variable length so the skipper could change the depth of the nets below the surface according to how high up the herring shoals were swimming. 2. A **stopper** (q.v.) or **leg** (q.v.), on an otter trawl. 3. A **seizing** (q.v.).

Strut: a Dan Leno post on a **Danish seine** (q.v.).

Sucker-fish: a species of leech, *Pontobdella muricata*, infesting rays and sometimes found referred to as *skate leech*.

Sue: to exude, or ooze out. The word was mainly used in connection with leaving salted fish or salted meat in fresh water for a short length of time, in order to draw some of the salt out prior to cooking. It probably derives from the Latin *sudare*, meaning "to sweat".

Summer boat: a sailing-and-pulling lifeboat, which was used during the finer months of the year. It was of lighter build and carried more sail than a **winter boat** (q.v.).

Summer sails: 1. Lighter sails, used on vessels during the finer months of the year. 2. Older sails, which might not stand up to the rigours of winter weather, but which were adequate for less taxing conditions.

Sunk-nets: drift-nets made of hemp, which had the **warp** (q.v.) floated up above them. The fibre was heavy enough to make the meshes hang correctly in the water. With the development of the lighter cotton nets, the warp had to be secured below so as to act as a weighting agent.

Surveyor: a Board of Trade official (or someone suitably qualified acting as agent) who carried out safety inspections on vessels prior to the start of a fishing voyage.

Swale: the term used when drift-nets and ropes got carried by wind and tide under the stern of a vessel, often fouling the propeller. The word is probably a variant of *sway* and first appeared during the early nineteenth century.

Swallowtail flag: a mast-head pennant with two tails or streamers, comparable with the deep fork of the tail of the bird.

Sweeps: large oars, used for rowing sailing drifters and smacks out of harbour in adverse weather conditions (usually, the lack of a fair wind). In Lowestoft and Great Yarmouth, Great Eastern Railway Company paddle-tugs were available for towing services, but a fee was charged.

Swell: the heaving motion of the sea which is detectable visually on the surface, but present also well below. A heavy swell could make life difficult and unpleasant on board – dangerous even, as referred to in the folksong, *Threescore and Ten* (see Appendix 2).

Swept clean: see **Clean-swept**.

Swill: a large, double-compartment wicker basket, with slightly bulbous sides, used for handling herrings in Great Yarmouth and neighbouring Gorleston only. It held two-thirds of a cran of herrings (almost nineteen stones by weight). In view of the shape, the name may originally have been a variant of "swell". The *Time and Tide Museum*, in Blackfriars Road, Great Yarmouth, has an excellent collection of all kinds of artifacts, photographs and records associated with the local herring industry.

Swim: the term used for herrings rising from the seabed towards the surface.

Swim up: an expression that is synonymous with **swim.**

Swimming-fish: a term used by trawlermen for certain demersal species, such as cod, haddock, hake, whiting etc., which live just above the seabed. This was to distinguish them from flatfish, such as plaice, dabs, sole, turbot and brill, which live on the bottom itself.

Swing/swinger/swing-on: a specially made section of a steam drifter's warp at the end nearest the boat. It ran from the **rope-room** (q.v.), round the capstan, as far as the stem-end net, and was made of the best manilla fibre. This gave the strength and elasticity needed for the point of maximum strain on the whole fleet of nets.

Swipe: to row (or sail) along a length of coastline, fairly close to shore, dragging a grapnel behind the boat, with the intention of hooking anchors which had been lost from other vessels. The recovery and re-sale of these was able to produce useful extra income for beachmen and longshoremen alike. The word is almost certainly a variant of *sweep*.

Swum-nets: cotton drift-nets, which had the **warp** (q.v.) secured beneath them – the opposite method of rigging **sunk-nets** (q.v.), as described above.

T

Taffrail: the gunwale/rail around the stern of a vessel. The word is a variant spelling of *tafferel*, which was the original form used in the early seventeenth century.

Take a sea: to meet a heavy swell broadside on (cf. **ship a sea**).

Take away: the term used of herring shoals moving from one area to another.

Take in: to give board and lodging to Scottish shore personnel, who came down to Great Yarmouth and Lowestoft every autumn to process the catches of herring taken by their own drifters and by the local East Anglian craft. Seaside landladies were able to extend their period of activity and ordinary families could also earn extra money by housing the visitors (stories are told of children either being sent to grandparents while Scottish people were in the house or even being put in garden sheds to make their rooms available). The working clothes of the **gutting-girls** (q.v.) were so impregnated with herring oil that their hosts often lined the walls of the hallways and the rooms in which they were lodged with oilcloth or brown paper, to absorb the grease and protect the underlying wallpaper or paint. When the Scottish fishermen and curing personnel left to go home at the end of the season (early-mid December), they spent a lot of money in both towns, buying Christmas presents for their families.

Take off: an expression very similar in meaning to **take away**. It refers to fish leaving a particular area of the sea for another and applied especially to pelagic species.

Take up: to draw the wages or payment due at the end of a fishing voyage.

Takle: a *tackle*. In other words, a pulley-block with its accompanying sheet or rope. The word was always given the pronunciation shown here.

Tally: 1. To count herrings or mackerel by hand, in **warps** (q.v.). 2. A paper label, with a fish merchant's name on it, which was placed on a kit or box of fish after it had been sold at auction in order to indicate ownership.

Tan: 1. To preserve drift-nets with **cutch** (q.v.). The term harks back to the time when oak or ash bark (which produced the *tanning* agent for curing leather) was used. 2. To treat sails (especially new ones) with a mixture of red ochre, horse-fat and seawater.

Tan-copper: a large, brick-built cistern with fire-hole beneath, adjacent to a **net-store** (q.v.) or even constructed onto one end, in which drift-nets were boiled in cutch.

Tan jumper: the brown **slop** (q.v.) customarily worn at one time by Lowestoft fishermen, which had been dyed in the agent used to preserve sails.

Tanner organs: scallops – most notably, the Great Scallop (*Pecten maximus*). The shell could be anything up to six inches long and the bivalve's culinary worth was well recognised. The term itself probably does not reflect the value of scallops commercially (a *tanner* being an old nickname for a sixpence), but may well refer to the shape of certain cinema and theatre organs of the Art Deco period. Ribbed shells were a popular decorative motif of the time and some electric organs had illuminated, shell-shaped backboards above the console. A sixpenny admission price to cinemas and dance-halls would also have been fairly common at the lower end of the entertainment scale.

Tanning-tank: a large, metal tank, carried by some of the bigger steam drifters on voyages away from home, in which the nets could be given preservative treatment.

Tar'us: a shed where ropes were stored. The term is a variant of *tar house* and may therefore refer to the substance used to render ropes resistant to the rotting effect of saltwater. It is also possible that it might have derived, originally, from *tow house*, thereby taking note of the hemp fibre from which ropes were made.

Task work: an alternative form of **test work** (q.v.).

Tell: to count herrings or mackerel (by hand) into **long hundreds** (q.v.), as the means of landing catches. The word derives from the Old English *tellan*, meaning "to count".

Test work: the work undertaken at the local workhouse, or in places further removed, in order to earn the **relief** (q.v.) payments made to unemployed people who were not entitled to **dole-money** (q.v.).

Thames mud: a smacksman's term for cocoa. It may perhaps be compared with an earlier term listed above: **brick dust** (q.v.). At least one of the Lowestoft smack skippers always insisted on the addition of mustard powder to the cocoa brewed up on his vessel, believing that it improved the flavour!

Thick (as guts): a term used to describe foggy weather.

Thick water: seawater full of plankton and herring oil, indicating shoal activity.

Thief-net: a bag-net which was rigged up along the side of a vessel, beneath incoming drift-nets, in order to catch herrings which fell from the meshes.

Third hand: the man below mate, in rank, on a Lowestoft smack or steam trawler.

Thole/thole-pin: one of a pair of wooden pegs set in a rowing boat's gunwale, to provide leverage for an oar. The word derives from the Old English *þol* or the Old Norse *þollr*, both meaning "a peg".

Thort: a variant pronunciation of *thwart* – a seat in a dinghy or rowing boat.

Thortcher-board: a plank which ran the width of a steam drifter, fore and aft of the hold, thereby acting as the end of the **kid** (q.v.) on both the port and starboard sides. *thortcher* is a corruption of "athwartship".

Threequarter-man: the member of a drifter's crew who was paid a threequarter- share.

Thrush: a coupling on a marine steam engine, which linked the piston to the crank.

Thwartcher-board: see **Thortcher-board**.

Tick: credit. Many fishing families lived on "tick" until the end of a voyage, when a settling-up would be made with the grocer, the baker etc. The word derives from the mark(s) made in the tradesmen's accounts to record the debts accrued by customers.

Ticket: a skipper's or mate's certificate of competence, allowing him to take command of a vessel.

Tickler: a chain rigged across the mouth of a trawl-net, in front of the **ground-rope** (q.v.) to cause disturbance to the sand on the seabed, thereby making the capture of flatfish more effective. Initially, the action was quite a gentle one (especially on beam trawls) – hence the name. However as time went on, *ticklers* became heavier and heavier, in order to "dig" flatfish from the bottom, terminating in the great chain-mats used by modern beam-trawlers – gear which has done considerable damage to fishing grounds all over the North Sea and in other parts of the world.

Tide about: to work the changes of the tide, when trawling, so as to attain the maximum number of shoots and hauls.

Tier: a layer of herrings in a Scotch-cure barrel.

Tiller: the helm of a sailing vessel. The word is first recorded in this sense during the 1620s and would seem to have derived from the Old French *telier*, meaning "a weaver's beam".

Tins: aluminium boxes for packing herrings in, on board ship. They were about two feet long, by fourteen inches wide, by eight inches deep, and each one held about four to four and a half stones of fish. Their use became widespread after the Second World War.

Tissot: a strong rope, made of **bass** (q.v.), which was attached to the warp on a fleet of drift-nets, at the end nearest the boat (by means of a rolling hitch), and made fast to the bow. Once this had been done, it took the strain of all the nets and ropes.

Titler: a **tickler chain** (q.v.).

Tits: sea anemones – especially *Actinia equina* (the Beadlet Anemone). The analogy is with female breasts, the shape being roughly comparable when the tentacles are withdrawn.

Tits-and-stones: *sea anemones* which attached themselves to stones on the seabed. These were trawled up from time to time in different parts of the North Sea, but fishermen were usually vague in their description of them. The most likely variety would seem to be *Sagartia troglodytes decorata*.

Titty-totty: very small. The first element may well derive from Scandinavian origins, with the second one thrown in as a makeweight. *Tit* was a word used during the medieval and early modern periods to indicate something small - e.g. *titlark, titmouse, tit-bit.*

Tom Wright's titty ones: small plaice. The reference here is to a well-known Pakefield smack skipper, who fished a particular ground somewhere out to the east of Lowestoft and often landed small plaice. These were popular with the **frying trade** (q.v.), because of their cheapness and palatability.

Tommy Hunter: a fishing vessel's mizzen mast forestay (especially used with reference to steam drifters). Exactly who Tommy Hunter was has never been explained.

Tongues: the smallest, eatable size of soles. Given the shape of the fish, the comparison is an obvious one to make.

Toppers: medium-sized plaice. The term probably refers to the good eating qualities of this class of fish. The bigger that plaice grow, the less succulent they become.

Top up: to fill up barrels of pickled herrings after settling had taken place.

Torbay sole: the Witch (*Glyptocephalus cynoglossus*). Given the northerly range of this fish (especially its presence off Faeroe and the coast of Norway), it is difficult to see a direct connection with south Devon – though, undoubtedly, the species was caught off its coasts.

Torn-bellies: herrings caught on the summer voyages to Shetland and North Shields, which burst easily because of their high oil content.

Tosher: a small sailing trawler or **smack** (q.v.), crewed by three or four men instead of the usual five. Three tended to be the summer crew, four the number employed during the winter. The origin of the word (which was also applied to someone who scavenged in the Victorian sewers of London) cannot be accurately defined.

Tow: to pull a trawl.

Tow-dinger: a tow-foresail. The *dinger* element, as used here, may indicate size and strength.

Tow-foresail: a large foresail, which was rigged on sailing drifters and on some of the early steamboats, to give extra speed in light winds. It was sheeted well aft on the vessel. The word *tow*, although not strictly correct in its usage, does serve to give a sense of forward motion.

Towing along: the act of trawling, whether by sail or by steam-power.

Towing-block: the metal case which held the warps of an **otter trawl** (q.v.) together, while the gear was in use.

Towing-post: a stout wooden pillar set amidships on a **smack** (q.v.), to which the warp was secured while the gear was being towed.

Trademark: an individual curer's name, stencilled on a barrel of Scotch pickled herrings, which served as a guarantee of the quality of the contents. It usually doubled with the official **Crown Brand** (q.v.) mark.

Trapstick: an iron rod which kept the mouth of a **thief-net** (q.v.) open and in position on the side of a steam drifter.

Trawl: a triangular-shaped bag-net, varying in size, which was dragged along the seabed to catch bottom-dwelling species. It was also rigged at times to operate further up in the water. Its first appearance is recorded in legislation of 1376 (when it was cited in Thames-side communities as causing serious damage to fish spawn and fry), and it was referred to as the *wondyrchoun* – literally, "a marvellous device".

Trawl dock: the basin lying alongside Waveney Road which housed the Lowestoft trawling fleet, as opposed to the vessels engaged in herring fishing (which used the Waveney Dock). It was greatly enlarged in 1892 to accommodate the increasing number of vessels involved in trawling.

Trawl-head: a large, forged, iron, stirrup-shaped hoop (one of a pair) on a beam trawl, which supported the beam and helped to keep the mouth of the net open.

Trawler band: the radio wavelength dedicated for use by British fishing vessels.

Trial trip: the test-run on which a new fishing vessel had the engine put through its paces and the compass set. Before the First World War, it was customary for the owner(s), the crew and the men who had built the boat to go on board (often accompanied by family members) and enjoy the outing. Harry Jenkins, a well-known Lowestoft photographer of the time, took many a picture of a vessel loaded up with people in their "Sunday-best" facing the camera. Such practice today would be deemed a health-and-safety nightmare!

Trick out: to spread fishing nets out, prior to inspecting them for damage.

Trimmer: 1. The second engineer on a steam trawler, who was responsible for keeping the furnace supplied with coal from the bunkers. The specific meaning of *trim* with regard to stowing and moving coal on board a ship dates from the 1790s. 2. A general term for a young crewman on board a steam trawler, who did all kinds of odd jobs in addition to his fishing duties.

Trip: 1. A single fishing excursion in and out of port. 2. The catch of fish resulting from such an excursion. It was common at one time to refer to a vessel's "trip o' fish", especially if it was a smack.
Triple: a triple-expansion, reciprocating steam engine.
Trow: a trough. This pronunciation was very common in East Anglia at one time.
Truck: The top of a mast – or, more precisely, the circular cap fixed there, with holes bored for halyards to run through.
Trunk: 1. To convey catches from fishing vessels to a **mother ship** (q.v.). The term was particularly associated with the Dogger Bank trawling fleets of the 1880s. 2. A stout wooden case (of about five to six stones capacity, or more) used to carry fish, in this kind of operation. 3. A sturdily built rowing boat used in trunking.
Trunking: the operation as described immediately above.
Tub: a sawn-off barrel or cask, with rope nailed around the top for sitting comfort, which served for toilet requirements on board ship. This was kept up on deck in as sheltered a place as possible – usually somewhere aft. An alternative to this (in fine weather only!) was to sit on the gunwale and "go over the side". On steam vessels, it was possible to go down into the engine-room, squat over a coal shovel and throw the faeces into the furnace. During the 1920s, both steam drifters and trawlers began to have closets built into them near the cabin.
Tubs: a disparaging term for fishing vessels which had seen better days. The shape of such craft was taken as being analogous with that of a bath – though the water they held down below was caused by leaking, not deliberate filling!
Turk's head: a special knot tied in the end of ropes and **tissots** (q.v.) to prevent slipping. It was supposed to resemble a turban in shape – hence the name.
Turk's knot: exactly the same as **Turk's head**.
Turn: 1. The twist in the strands of a rope. 2. The act of passing a rope or line once round a vertical or horizontal timber (a mast, spar etc.).
Turn in: to go to bed, on board ship.
Tusk: the Torsk (*Brosme brosme*) – a member of the cod group of fishes, caught mainly in the waters of Iceland and Faeroe.
Twenty-five holers: hard tack biscuits, which had that particular number of pin-pricks in the surface. These *sea biscuits* (as they were also called) were

The Lowestoft **Trawl Dock or Trawl Basin** in October 1981, with a number of trawlers. The harbour entrance is in the foreground with the Yacht Basin on the left and the turn into the Waveney Dock on the right. Through the bridge is the Inner Harbour or Lake Lothing.

made from flour, salt and water and baked slowly, so as to produce long-lasting qualities – as well as a range of pejorative nicknames from the men who ate them! They were a long-established staple food at sea, going back centuries, and could be made palatable (when eaten in conjunction with other food) by first soaking in salt-water and then heating up in the oven – having first been tapped sharply on a hard surface to encourage the self-evacuation of any grubs or weevils that had burrowed in! There is an incidental, ironically humorous reference to them in the folksong, *The Female Cabin Boy*. See also, **Cooper's rusks.**

Twenty-minute swimmers: traditional Norfolk dumplings, made of flour, salt and water mixed together and cooked for twenty minutes (by simmering in water) in a greased saucepan or steamer. See also, **Light duff**.

Twist (a): a mid-twentieth century term used to describe some of the under-hand business dealings carried out on the Lowestoft fish market (and in other places) with regard to the purchase and sale of catches. The use of the word, in portraying manipulation of some kind, was common at one time – but is no longer so much in fashion. One of the writer's respondents, who spent his whole working-life on the Lowestoft market, was in no doubt as to the industry's seamier side: "The whole o' the fish-trade wuz a twist from start t' finish!"

Two-swims: herrings which were left in the meshes after a look-on and hauled later, thereby being enmeshed for two tides.

U

Unbend: to take the seizings and strops off drift-nets.
Underfoots: the **perk boards** (q.v.) on steam drifters.
Underlay: to take up a drifting position on the windward side of a vessel which was already fishing, thereby attempting to anticipate the shoal.
Under-run: the term used of a **longshore boat** (q.v.) being rowed up and down the line of its nets, with one man taking herrings from the meshes and watching the movements of the fish. This was sometimes done if a heavy catch looked likely, because too many herrings coming aboard a small vessel could cause it to capsize.
Unlaying: the term used for the strands at the end of a rope becoming

separated. Whipping it with twine was the best preventative measure.

Unrig: to undo the **norsels** (q.v.) and set up drift-nets anew.

Up: southwards. This was an expression used of the North Sea, based on the fact that the flood tide runs in a southerly direction. Hence, a Lowestoft smacksman would always refer to "runnin' up to London River", if a trawling trip was made to grounds off the Thames Estuary.

Up-along: a trawling area off the Suffolk and Essex coast, in the area of the Gabbard and Galloper banks. It was popular with smacks and drifter-trawlers in the early months of the year, to provide good fishing, with a variety of species being caught. *Up* derives from the southerly direction taken by the vessels; *along* refers to the grounds being relatively close to land (about twenty miles out).

Up-through-bridge: the inner harbour at Lowestoft, which was reached through a road bridge that swung open horizontally. Its replacement today is a double-leaf bascule.

V

Vat: a concrete-lined tank, in the floor of curing-premises, in which herrings were steeped in brine – sometimes as a prelude to smoking; and, on other occasions, as a method of cure in its own right.

Vatted herring(s): fish that had been cured in the manner described immediately above.

Vice-consul: a man who undertook (if needed) to represent the interests of foreign nationals in port. He was usually someone already involved in the fish-trade (e.g. a merchant or vessel-owner), with the requisite experience to act effectively. Towards the end of the nineteenth century, three men served the following European countries, grouped as shown and very much representing the totality of Lowestoft's overseas trade and fishing links: Germany, the Netherlands, Sweden and Norway; France; Denmark, Russia and Spain. At a later period, after the Second World War, certain of the Lowestoft fishing companies undertook consular duties when required from offices located on Waveney Road, facing the trawl dock.

Voyage: a fishing season (usually of some weeks' duration) of a local nature or one that was undertaken in other parts of the British Isles. The term tended to be applied to herring or mackerel fishing rather than to trawling – but it was also used in the latter context.

W

Wag it/wag off: to play truant from school (see also, **Play the wag**). A favourite place for Lowestoft boys to go, when absent from their places of education, was the Fish Market. Pennies were to be earned there from **running up** (q.v.), doing useful small jobs about the place or from scavenging surplus and discarded fish. This situation prevailed up until the outbreak of the Second World War – but the post-war period ushered in a different world, with the Market less of an attraction to young lads (for all kinds of reasons) and with different social factors in play generally. Having said that, however, one of the writer's own students in a Lowestoft high school (during the 1980s) spent much of his final year down on the Fish Market doing a part-time job. He even came into school on one occasion to ask his teacher to act as referee for him in his attempt to open a bank account, in which to place the money he was earning!

Wale: 1. The intertwined rim of a wicker basket. 2. The raised "belt" on the outside of a vessel's hull, midway between rail and water-level. The word derives from the Old English *walu*, meaning "a ridge of land".

Waleman: the crew member of a steam drifter who was paid a threequarter and half-quarter share, who had specific duties on the fore-deck and who assisted the hawseman to shoot the net-rope.

Walings: the two landing stages on the Lowestoft fish market. The lower one (forming a ledge, as it did) particularly fitted the meaning of *ridge* as given in **Wale** above (see illustration on page 180).

Walk about: to be out of work, unemployed. The image conveyed in the expression, of lack of focus and direction in life, is an evocative one.

Walking meat: an expression used by some fishermen to describe the old, tough meat (usually beef) sometimes taken on board ship among the provisions. "If they'd left the hoofs on, it would've walked aboard!" was a remark made more than once by certain of the writer's respondents.

Wally/wolly: a wooden bar, used for helping to straighten out tangled driftnets. "Send for Wally!" used to be the cry on board, when the device was needed. The origin of the term is not known.

Warehouse: the term used for the Gorleston beach companies' headquarters and storage premises.

Warp: 1. The master rope for towing trawl gear or securing drift-nets. The word is often encountered in late medieval and early modern probate inventories (for people living in coastal communities) as *warrope*. It derives originally from the Old English *wearp* and undoubtedly has the sense (as used in weaving) of threads or fibres being twisted and extended lengthways. 2. A count of four herrings or mackerel (two in each hand), as a means of telling out long hundreds. Again, the word is encountered in medieval usage, meaning a count of four fish.

Warp round: to work a sailing vessel around a harbour's quays, using a rope and capstan, as a means of getting it out of port.

Washed herring(s): herrings stripped of their scales, which rendered them less saleable at market. This sometimes happened when a drifter had a very heavy haul of fish and the crew were not able to stow all of the catch properly. It could also result from a vessel rolling a lot in heavy weather and water getting into the fish-hold.

Wash(ing): a quantity of whelks (usually a sackful), to serve as bait for **longlines** (q.v.). The variety used was the Common Whelk (*Buccinum undatum*) and it was well regarded by fishermen because, once impaled, it held firmly on the hook. Most of the whelks used in Lowestoft came down by rail from Boston, in Lincolnshire, having been caught in the Wash. The term *washing* had nothing to do with this part of the North Sea; it referred to the shellfish being washed clean of sand and sediment before being packed into sacks for transportation.

Washing-day cake: a cake that was cheaply made at the beginning of the week (Monday being the traditional washing-day) from marrow-bone fat, flour, sugar and currants. People who didn't have their own oven at home would take the mix to a nearby baker's shop, where it would be cooked for a small fee (usually a penny or so) – much the same kind of practice as that referred to by Dickens in *A Christmas Carol*, with regard to the Cratchit family's festive goose.

Washing ma(u)nd: a basket used in smokehouses for rinsing fish, prior to curing them.

Watch: a turn of duty in the wheelhouse of a steam drifter or trawler, or at the tiller of a smack.

Watchman: 1. The man on duty in the wheelhouse of a vessel, or at the tiller (the term was used especially of the night watches). 2. A man who kept fishing craft under scrutiny when they lay in harbour (either because they observed the custom of not fishing on a Sunday or because the weather was too bad to go out), to make sure that nothing was stolen or interfered with on board. He was usually a retired fisherman.

Water-boats: small fishery-patrol vessels.

Water-tube boiler: a boiler in which steam was raised by having the water running through tubes which were surrounded by fire – the opposite in principle to the normal type of boiler. This was a faster way of raising steam, but such boilers were more expensive to construct. Very few fishing vessels had them.

Ways: wooden timbers used in a shipyard to assist the passage of a vessel from its resting position into the water. Sometimes used (mistakenly) as a substitute for **skeets** (q.v.).

Wear away: to release the warps on trawling gear once the net was over the side of the vessel.

Weather-law: the term used of when drift-nets were shot across the direction of the wind, not straight before it (which was the usual practice).

Weather-shore: a shore with the wind blowing off it, seawards, which was able to offer shelter to vessels in rough conditions.

Weather-tide: a tide running against the direction of the wind, which could create a good deal of turbulence (depending on the strength of the wind).

Weever: the Greater Weever (*Trachinus draco*). This was often trawled up and formed that part of a vessel's catch which constituted the crew's **stocker bait** (q.v.). The main risk in handling it was the venom injected by the front dorsal fin. This could inflict a very painful wound to the hands. The Lesser Weaver (*Trachinus vipera*) was not much encountered by trawlers, but bathers on the Lowestoft south beach were (and still are) made aware of its presence from time to time during the late summer and early autumn, when they stepped on one as it lay half buried in the shallows. Again, the front dorsal fin inflicts an excruciating sting to the bottom of the foot.

Weighing: a hundredweight of fish. The term is a variant of *wey* (deriving from Old English *wæġ*, meaning "a balance" or "weight") which, in the medieval and early modern periods, was a measure of weight for dry goods that varied from commodity to commodity.

Well: a storage space below decks. It might refer to the **fish-hold** (q.v.), or even a compartment within it. For an explanation of the origin of the word, see **After-well**.

Welsh Hard: anthracite. This was used as the fuel in tan-copper furnaces because of the heat it produced.

Went foreign: the term used of a fishing vessel that was sold to a purchaser from the mainland of Europe (or from anywhere else in the world) and which then moved to a new operational base abroad.

Went through: became bankrupt. The term was used particularly of fishing companies and Scottish curers who got into serious financial trouble during the 1920s and 30s.

Westerly: a metaphorical term used for someone being treated to a drink in a public house (westerly winds bring moisture!).

West'ard: the fishing voyages made to Devon and Cornwall, especially drift-netting for mackerel out of Newlyn (February-March) and trawling for soles at Padstow (March-May). The word is a simple variation of Westward.

Whaleback: a fishing vessel which had a whale-deck for'ad. The upper surface of this structure was often convex, which suggested the shape or profile of a whale's back.

Whale-deck: deck space which is roofed over (usually for'ad), to afford protection from the elements. Its rounded upper profile bore comparison with the cetacean's back.

Wheelhouse: a superstructure raised above the level of the decks, which contained the steering gear and other equipment necessary for navigating the vessel. It was integral with the engine-room casing and, in the earlier vessels, often located aft-side of the funnel. Later models always had it in front.

Wheelhouse skipper: a skipper who did not involve himself in the hard work of shooting and hauling nets, but who watched (and sometimes controlled) proceedings from the wheelhouse. Other masters made themselves very much working members of the crew – something that was always appreciated on board by the other crew members.

Whiffler: a device for regulating the draught on a steam engine's furnace. The word *whiffle* is one which relates to the wind and means "to blow in puffs", or slight gusts.

Whilk(s): whelk(s).

Whilk-cracker: someone in a longliner's crew (usually, a junior member) who broke the whelk shells and got the bait ready to be hooked on.

Whip: to lash twine around a join in a rope or at its end (to prevent the strands from unravelling).

Whips: immature Conger Eels (*Conger conger*). The slender build, relative to the length, is what gave rise to the name.

Whistle up a wind: to whistle on board a vessel, while at sea. This was greatly frowned upon, as many fishermen believed that a gale would be the result of such musical efforts. Some of the older hands even disliked the practice when a boat was berthed in harbour.

White-elephants: fishing vessels which never earned much money – a term that may be taken as analogous with **crab-boats** (q.v.).

White fish: trawlfish species – especially those such as cod, haddock and whiting.

White herrings: pickled herrings (i.e. those produced by **Scotch cure**).

White horses: broken, turbulent water above sandbanks. The term is one in general use and conjures up images of animals at full gallop, with streaming manes. It can also refer to the whipping-up of the sea's surface by high winds, creating foaming wave-tops and blown spray.

White nets: 1. New cotton drift-nets, before they had been **tanned** (q.v.). 2. Longshore drift-nets which had been given preservation treatment which did not darken them. A number of fishermen believed that they were more effective at catching herrings and sprats than nets which had been tanned – perhaps because of a belief that they were less visible in the water. However, when either of these species shoaled, the colour of the nets probably mattered very little.

Whitebait: immature herrings and sprats (the two often swam together). Fried whole, heads included, they have long featured on restaurant menus as a starter-dish.

Whitenin': the Whiting (*Merlangius merlangus*). This species was never very highly valued by some people because it was smaller than either cod or haddock and it was, in some cases, even relegated to the status of cat-food. Other people (including many fishermen themselves) rated it more highly, finding it entirely palatable – especially if eaten fresh on board ship.

Widders an' Orphans (The): a local expression for the Lowestoft Fishermen's Widows' and Orphans' Benevolent Fund, which was formed in 1879 to assist the dependents of men lost or deceased at sea on Lowestoft fishing vessels. The charity is still in existence, though its name was changed in 1996 to the Lowestoft Fishermen's and Seafarers' Benevolent Society – in recognition of the diminished fishing operation in the port and the fact that a number of local seamen were connected with servicing the North Sea offshore oil and gas industries.

Wigging (in): listening in to other skippers' conversations on the radio's trawler band. This was done in the hope of learning where good catches of fish were to be had. The term is a variant of **earwigging** (q.v.).

Will-ducks/willies: Guillemots (*Uria aalge*). The *duck* reference derives from the way that these birds sat on the surface of the water, riding the swell, and the "guille" element of the bird's name may be taken as rhyming with "willy". Interestingly, the word *guillemot* itself has been identified as a variant form of the French *Guillaume*, meaning William!

Winch: the horizontally mounted device on board a trawler (placed in front of the wheelhouse) used for hauling the net. It was driven by steam for many years, before being superseded by hydraulic action after the adoption of diesel propulsion by fishing vessels.

Wind-bladder: the swim-bladder of a fish – an important organ for maintaining buoyancy.

Wind-bound: prevented from fishing by high winds.

Wind-drieds: gutted herrings which were rubbed with salt, then hung out to cure by drying in the fresh air.

Windlass: a horizontal winch on board a smack, used for running out and hauling in the **bowsprit** (q.v.).

Wing-doors: an alternative term for **lee-boards** (q.v.).

Wing-end: the mouth of a trawl net (the opposite extremity to the cod-end).

Wings: 1. The side-spaces or compartments in a steam drifter, either side of the fish hold. 2. The extended sections of a trawl net along its sides. On a **beam trawl** (q.v.), these were beneath the square and between the beam and the belly. On an **otter trawl** (q.v.), there were two pairs: the upper ones were between the square and the legs/bridles; the lower ones were between the belly and the legs/bridles. 3. The enlarged pectoral fins of rays and skate.

Winter boat: a **sailing-and-pulling lifeboat** (q.v.) of sturdy build, used during the winter months.

Winter herrings: small, **full** (q.v.), North Sea herrings caught off the Norfolk/Suffolk coast during February.

Wires: the warps used on otter trawls (made of high-tensile, twisted, steel strands).

Witch(es): a type of flatfish (see **Torbay sole**).

Wolded ground-ropes: ground-ropes for trawls, made by winding sacking around the wire core and then putting **rounding** (q.v.) over this. They were highly rated for holding close to the seabed and catching flatfish (especially soles).

Wolders: mackerel caught in the autumn on the *Cromer Wold* fishing-ground, off the north-east coast of Norfolk, about five or six miles out from land. During the late nineteenth century and the years leading up to the First World War, the season was an important one in Lowestoft particularly.

Woodbine funnel: a slender smoke-stack on early steam drifters, which supposedly had a similarity of shape to the famous cigarette.

Woodbines: early steam drifters, which had slender funnels and **Elliot pot** (q.v.) engines.

Woodlouse-things: crustaceans of the order *Isopoda* (and therefore commonly referred to as *isopods*), which were observed by vessels **longlining** (q.v.) out of Milford Haven as predating on whiting and ling particularly. The species in question may have been *Sphaeroma serratum*.

Work-O!: identical to "**Busky-O!**" – the call to begin hauling nets on a drifter.

Workhouse ships: Dutch drifters and trawlers, with a number of youngsters in the crew, which stayed at sea for long periods and processed catches on board. The term reflects the hard life on board.

Wrapper/wropper: a fisherman's neckerchief (sometimes made of black silk). This item of clothing proved useful at times as an improvised bag, in which to take fish home at the end of a voyage. Claims have been made that a wrapper could carry as many as a hundred herrings.

Wrongs: the bent boughs of large oak trees, which were used for making the frames of wooden fishing vessels. Master shipwrights identified these on the estates where oak was purchased and marked the trees they wished to be felled. This sense of the word, meaning "crooked" or "curved", can be traced back to 1613.

Wymewden: the pronunciation used in Lowestoft and Great Yarmouth to represent the Dutch port of Ijmuiden (deriving from Ymuiden, a variant form of the name).

Y

Yarco: a fisherman from Great Yarmouth. There is a fencing company, based in neighbouring Gorleston, which uses the name – apparently, in some kind of recognition of days gone by.

Yard: a spar on which a topsail was set, on a smack. Various North European languages have words of similar appearance, meaning "a rod", from which the term may have derived: e.g. *ġerd* (Old English), *jerde* (Old Frisian) and *gerdia* (Old Swedish).

Yaw: to deviate from a course, usually because of faulty steering.

Yoll: a yawl. This type of long, clinker-built craft (powered by lugsail or oars) was used by the **beach companies** (q.v.) for salvage work and rescue. The pronunciation here may well reflect the Dutch origins of the word: *jolle*.

Younker: the Great Yarmouth term for the **cast-off** (q.v.) on board a steam drifter. The word not only reflects the youthfulness of this particular crew member; it derives from the Middle Dutch *jonckher*, meaning "young lord", and may also be compared with the German *junkher*.

Yowler(s): young herrings, larger in size than **seeds** (q.v.).

Z

Zulu: a Scottish sailing drifter, with a cut-away or raked stern. It was a bigger and faster version of the **Fifie** (q.v.) and got its name from the fact that it was developed in 1878-9, at the same time as the Zulu War was taking place in South Africa.

The great fish markets of Great Yarmouth and now increasingly Lowestoft are of the past, but the words and phrases of the sea-going and shore based men and women are recorded here and on the original tapes lodged with the Suffolk Record Office.

Appendix 1
Superstition and the Fisherman

The collection of superstitions which follows is not seen, in any way, as definitive. It simply records a number of the more commonly held beliefs once current in East Anglian fishing communities. Not all of them were peculiar to fishermen only; some had (and may still have) currency among seafarers in general, while others can be traced well inland. But no matter how extensive their area of circulation, all of them are interesting for what they tell us of the human mind and the way it works when faced with natural powers beyond either its understanding or its control.

The last factor is crucial when considering superstition of any kind. How does anyone explain the inexplicable? – arguably, with truth on very rare occasions and with plausible mumbo-jumbo the rest of the time. Those of us living today have the benefit of the scientific discovery of the last hundred years particularly, but what about people living in times when fewer explanations were available? Take the case of a thunderstorm. How many contemporary British citizens could explain exactly what happens to cause one? And even if the physics are understood, does that in any sense diminish the awesome power unleashed during a tempest?

The forces of nature are always at their most imposing when at their angriest, and probably no one sees this more often and more directly than the seafarer. The closeness of contact with the elements not only breeds respect for the ocean; it also makes a person look constantly for signs of adverse conditions, even perhaps when they are not present. Such a sense of foreboding is undoubtedly the origin of some of the superstitions recorded below. They are (if we like to think of them in this manner) omens of what could happen, rather than what had – but that in no way diminishes their hold on people.

If anything, the opposite is true. Most of us have something deep within us which responds to the mysterious, or even (on occasions) the obviously occult. Rationality plays no part in the feelings; it is something that is there within us – a legacy from our primitive past, which centuries of progress and improvement have not succeeded in eradicating. Thus it is that none of us should have too much trouble in following the line of thought that produced these superstitions, several of which function on the principle of sympathetic magic, where an action or deed can assume a good or evil outcome simply by association or analogy.

1. **Breaking eggshells.** This was always done after the cracking of eggs in cooking, because it was believed that half an eggshell could provide a witch or an evil spirit with a craft in which to put to sea and there cause havoc. Similarly, after a boiled egg had been eaten, the shell was either broken or turned upside-down in the egg-cup and a hole poked through it. The writer was taught the latter practice, as a very small boy, by his maternal grandparents – and this was well inland, in a Norfolk village situated between Bungay and Harleston.

2. **Never launch a vessel on a Friday.** This custom was always strictly adhered to with newly-built craft. Neither was a fishing-boat's keel ever laid down on a Friday. Both practices were believed to bring bad luck, even to the point of total loss of both vessel and crew. The taboos surrounding Friday probably have their origin in pre-Reformation times, when Friday was held sacred as the day on which Jesus Christ died and common, everyday tasks were often kept to a minimum.

3. **Never begin a fishing voyage on a Friday.** Another of the common superstitions regarding Friday. What is meant specifically here by *voyage* is a major fishing time-of-year, such as the local autumn herring season, or the winter migration of East Anglian crews round to Newlyn to catch mackerel. Once the venture was under way, there was no threat in boats leaving port on a Friday because they were now making *trips* – and that was completely different matter.

4. **Women on board ship.** This was anathema to most fishermen – one of the things they thought most likely to cause a vessel to sink. The idea of

women representing a destructive force is to be found the whole world over – a reversal, really, of their biological creativity and with undertones of the male feeling sexually threatened by them. It is no accident that the old stories have Eve plucking the fruit and Pandora opening the box!

5. **Washing clothes.** This was never done on the day that a fisherman left home to start a voyage. To do so would undoubtedly prove fatal and cause the man to drown, the domestic task being synonymous with "washing his life away" – a good example of sympathetic magic in operation.

6. **Watching a loved one depart.** This simple action was fraught with danger if the wife or children watched the man of the house, or any other relative, disappear from sight at the end of the street, or round a corner, when starting off on a fishing voyage. It meant that he would never be seen again. The remedy was simple: you did not stand and watch him for any length of time after the goodbyes had been said.

7. **Dislike of clergymen.** Many local fishermen believed that to allow a minister of religion to step on board was bound to bring bad luck. This was not so much to do with losing the vessel itself as with causing poor catches to be had. The Bishop of Aberdeen caused an upset on the Lowestoft fish-market in the post-war period when he attempted to set foot on one of the local boats, in ignorance of local beliefs (Scottish fishermen did not share these, to the same degree). A notable exception to the rule was the Rev. A. D. Tupper-Carey, rector of St. Margaret's, Lowestoft, from 1901-10. He was so well thought of among the fishermen that he was welcome aboard any time and, on one occasion, he even sailed down to Shetland on a steam drifter for the summer herring voyage.

8. **Dislike of nuns.** Female clergy roused even stronger feelings than ordained ministers, combining both the traditional dislike of women and the suspicion felt towards people connected with organised religion. In fact, it wasn't unknown for Lowestoft fishermen to refuse to put to sea if they passed, or saw, a nun on their way to the harbour. And there was a good chance of their doing so if they lived in the southern part of town, because St. Mary's Convent stood at the top of Kirkley Cliff. The

only remedy, apparently, for warding off the ill luck caused by sighting a nun was to immediately touch some object made of iron. This was accompanied by the shout of "Cold iron!" or "Iron! Iron!" And if there were no gates, lamp-posts or fence railings conveniently to hand, the Blakeys or studs in the soles of boots would suffice. This belief in the efficacy of iron to counter a malign influence goes back to the Anglo-Saxon period at least, and may be even older.

9. **Copper coins in fishing-net corks.** It was not unusual for the corks on drift-net headlines to be split at periodic intervals and have pennies or halfpennies inserted into the incisions. This served a dual purpose: the coins acted as weights along the headline, but they also functioned as good-luck charms in the sense of being an offering to the gods in exchange for a good catch.

10. **Wetting the nets.** Before a herring voyage commenced, many boat-owners used to have a small celebration in the yards of their net-stores. The success of the voyage was toasted in either beer or spirits, and a few drops of the particular beverage were sprinkled on the nets. Such a *libation* is both ancient in origin and thoroughly pagan.

11. **The number of drift-nets cast.** This was always an odd number, whether fishing for herring or mackerel, the reasoning being that "the extra net" would bring good luck. Hence, a drifter would shoot 75 nets, or 83, or 111 etc., depending on its size and fishing capacity.

12. **Buying a catch.** Religious feeling (or perhaps it would be more accurate to say pseudo-religious) manifested itself on board ship in the custom of throwing some pennies or halfpennies overboard before shooting drift-nets or trawls. This was ostensibly to "buy a catch" from The Almighty, working on the principle that nobody ever gets something for nothing.

13. **"Over for the Lord".** There were different versions of this utterance, made by the mate prior to the first net being cast - he being the crew member to perform this task on both sailing drifters and steam/diesel vessels. It was a prayer, really, for a good catch of herrings and it is said to derive from references in the Gospels to the hauls of fish made by certain

of the disciples in the Sea of Galilee – particularly the one mentioned in the last chapter of St. John, which is generally referred to as "the miraculous draught" (John 21. 4-8).

14. **Abusing the Almighty.** In the event of trawls or drift-nets coming up empty or with a poor catch, it was not unknown for some of the more blasphemous skippers to blame the Creator, whom they held directly responsible for their bad fortune, and invite him to come down and give an account of his actions. Some even used to go as far as to challenge him to a fight, in which (should he appear) he might expect to suffer some degree of bodily harm – and one particular smack's skipper was known to climb the mainmast brandishing a hand-axe.

15. **The King Herring.** Occasionally, an Allis Shad (*Alosa alosa*) would be shaken from the meshes of drift nets as they were being hauled. Because of its passing resemblance to the herring, and its larger size, it was always identified as a "shoal leader" and was therefore thrown back into the sea, to lead future shoals into the awaiting nets. The cry of "King Herring!" usually accompanied the act, not only to indicate the belief concerning the species, but to comment perhaps on the importance of herrings generally in the local economy.

16. **The October full moon.** Traditionally, East Anglian fishermen believed that the best catches of herring were taken at "October full", especially when that occurred about the middle of the month (or even later). Landing statistics bear this out, but it had nothing to do with any gravitational influence. It just happens that the southward movement of the shoals towards their spawning grounds in the English Channel peaked at about this time, before gradually diminishing throughout the month of November.

17. **Scrubbing the decks.** Some of the more old-fashioned skippers did not believe in their boats being *too* clean, because they reckoned that a certain amount of fish refuse lying around showed that a vessel was earning money. Too great an insistence, therefore, on cleanliness might well take away the luck needed to make paying hauls.

18. **Leaving deck-brooms on top of nets.** This was never done, either on board ship or at the quayside, and the reason for this is a perfect example of sympathetic magic. If a fisherman were so foolish as to do such a thing, then he was inviting disaster next time the nets were cast. They would, in all likelihood, be lost, because leaving a broom lying on top of them represented their being swept away.

19. **Leaving bunker-lids lying the wrong way up.** The metal lids that were set into the deck above the coal bunkers and fish-hold were not unlike small metal manhole covers to look at. When they were taken out, they always had to be placed on their backs, which then symbolised the hull of the vessel. If they were left lying the other way up, it was believed that this might cause the boat to turn turtle.

20. **Hatred of pigs.** These animals had a bad reputation among fishermen because (it is said) of the story of the Gadarene swine in the Gospels (Mark 5. 1-17; Luke 8. 26-36). The specific reference as to how the herd ran into the waters and drowned is said to have made fishermen very uneasy, though no doubt the reputation of the pig as a "dirty animal" also played its part. Not only were crew members forbidden to mention pigs on board ship (one particular substitute used was *Irish lambs*), some skippers also refused to carry bacon or pork among the boat's provisions. Another possible explanation of the unease surrounding the animal may be traced back to Celtic times, when a powerful British earth-goddess, Ceridwen, is said to have taken the form of a large black sow as one of her manifestations. Whatever the case, there were exceptions to the rule of taboo where pigs were concerned – a notable one being the Lowestoft trawler skipper, William "Oscar" Pipe, during the 1930s. He had the wheelhouse of his vessel, the *Blanche* (H 928), decorated with dried and varnished pigs' tails nailed around the top and with a head similarly treated set above the window. Such a flagrant disregard for tradition did not seem to have affected him unduly either, because he was a very successful operator.

21. **Dislike of other animals.** While pigs attracted the greatest ill-feeling, animals in general were often taboo in conversation on board ship. Rabbits gave cause for unease among some fishermen; so did cattle, horses and sheep; and even exotic creatures such as monkeys, elephants

and camels were frowned upon. When radio receiving-sets first began to be installed in the Lowestoft and Yarmouth fishing fleets during the 1920s and 30s, some of the skippers would switch them off as soon as they heard livestock market reports and the prices mentioned, for fear they might hear any forbidden animals referred to. In view of such feeling, it may seem strange that many vessels carried a cat (usually to control vermin) and that some skippers would often take their dogs to sea with them.

22. The Fiddle-fish. The Monkfish, or Angel Ray (*Squatina squatina*), was given this name because its shape supposedly resembled that of a violin. It was the custom on the Lowestoft sailing smacks, if one of them was trawled up, to nail it by its tail to the mizzen mast as a good luck charm. Sometimes, the fish had a lashing secured to its tail and it would then be thrown overboard for the boat to tow along on the journey back to port.

23. Rats. Everyone has heard the saying, "Rats always desert a sinking ship", and fishermen were no exception in believing this. Even so, the presence of these animals on board was something of a mixed blessing, so many drifters and trawlers carried a cat in order to keep the numbers down.

24. Whistling on board ship. This was strictly forbidden at sea, and even frowned upon in port, because it was believed to be a sure way of raising high winds and gales. Both the expulsion of air through the lips and the sound that this makes combine to create a perfect example of sympathetic magic at work.

25. Singing on board ship. This was disliked by some skippers, especially when at sea, because they thought that it would lead to poor catches. Herring fishermen particularly believed this.

26. Stirring tea with knives or forks. This might be done sometimes on board if a spoon wasn't immediately to hand, but it was a practice disapproved of by the older fishermen in particular, who saw it as a potential cause of trouble among crew members. *Stir with a knife; stir up strife.* That was one saying. Another went thus: *Stir with a fork; stir up talk.* And talk, in this case, meant arguments.

27. **The colour green.** This was another of the fisherman's great hates and a very bad omen indeed. Hence, no one wore green clothes of any kind on board ship and few boats were painted green. The superstition surrounding the colour is both ancient and widespread, for it is the so-called *fairy hue*, the Earth Mother's own personal tint – and, in seeming to represent the substance of life itself, it has long been held in awe. George Ewart Evans, over many years of collecting the oral history of the East Anglian farmworker, frequently encountered unease concerning the colour green.

28. **White-handled knives.** These were taboo also as far as some of the older fishermen were concerned and, whether for eating meals or gutting fish, were not allowed on board. The particular belief at work here was the association of white with death – the idea of its being the *corpse colour*. One of the writer's respondents, who worked on a motorised smack during the early 1950s, was compelled to throw a bone-handled gutting knife overboard as the vessel left Lowestoft harbour, and it was accompanied by a green jumper knitted for him by his fiancée!

29. **White stones.** These were disliked by many fishermen for the reason explained above and, if any were trawled up from the seabed, they were quickly thrown back. It was not unknown for some of the old smack skippers (and owners) to pick through the shingle ballast of a new vessel and discard as many white stones as they were able to.

30. **Ear-rings.** It was believed that the piercing of ears and the wearing of ear-rings was able to improve eyesight. The usual custom was to have only the left lobe done and to wear a single, gold ring therein. The practice seems to have penetrated well inland; the writer's maternal grandfather, a farmworker from the Acle area of Norfolk, always sported an ear-ring. He may well have had contemporaries, as a young man, who went fishing out of Great Yarmouth; while he was still an infant, his own father (from the village of Halvergate) had drowned during the 1890s working on a sailing drifter from the port.

31. **A baby's caul.** The membrane found on the heads of some new-born infants was regarded as a sovereign charm against drowning. High

prices were paid for cauls, which were usually carried somewhere about the person – often in a small bag hung round the neck on a drawstring. The most famous caul recorded is that mentioned in the first chapter of *David Copperfield*. The eponymous hero was born with one, which was advertised in the newspapers for the sum of fifteen guineas and, having failed to attract interest, was then raffled off locally. Dickens would have become well acquainted with maritime belief and practice during his visit to Great Yarmouth in 1848 and he was a master at incorporating regional culture into his novels. He may even have known that the caul was valued so highly because of its passing resemblance to the shape of a boat's hull. Here again, sympathetic magic is seen in operation: the analogy between the caul's shape and the safety that represents to someone who possesses one while at sea.

32. **Dying on the ebb tide.** It was widely held in fishing communities that a dying person would hold on to life until the tide turned from the flood to the ebb. Then he or she would depart this world. Again, there is a reference to this in *David Copperfield*, chapter 30, where Mr. Peggotty describes Barkis's passing to David (they are both present in the room, at his deathbed) in the following way: "He's a-going out with the tide."

33. **Seagulls.** These were believed to be the souls of drowned seafarers, which had assumed another form and could not leave the element that had caused their demise.

34. **Fairy-loaves.** These were fossilised sea urchins, which were sometimes found on cliff-faces and beaches. They were also known as *pharisee-loaves*, or *farcy-loaves*, and were regarded as symbols of good luck, often being taken into people's houses, varnished over and placed on mantle-pieces and shelves. Their shape, being roughly suggestive of a loaf of bread, led to the idea that those people who possessed them would never starve. The word "pharisee" (and its corruption, "farcy") derives originally from the Gaelic *fer-sidhean*, which literally means "fairy-men". George Ewart Evans has an illuminating piece about fairy-loaves in chapter 13 of *The Pattern Under the Plough*.

Fairy-loaves, a symbol of good luck for the fisherman.

35. **Hag-stones.** Any stone with a hole through the middle has long been regarded as lucky, especially as a charm against the depredations of witches and evil spirits. Many fishing vessels had them hanging up in either cabin or wheelhouse, or above the entrance to these, just as one might have expected to find them hanging over the doorway of a house. Again, there are details of the practice in chapter 18 of the book cited in no. 34 above.

36. **The all-seeing eye.** The *oculus* which is painted on the prow of many Mediterranean fishing craft was paralleled in East Anglian vessels of both the sail and steam eras by the ornamental hawse-pipe and accompanying maker's scroll. The hawse-pipe was the hole through which the anchor chain ran and it usually had a red surround, as well as a blue, wooden tampion for insertion when it was not being used. The maker's scroll was the particular shipbuilder's individual device, which was cut into the bow of a boat on both the port and starboard sides and then gilded. It always incorporated the hawse-pipe and formed a most attractive motif. The painting of an eye-like image on the bows of craft goes back to the times of ancient Egypt, when *the eye of Horus* was one of the most potent of all good-luck charms. No local vessel in East Anglia was reckoned complete without its builder's scroll, but it is debatable as to whether people at the time were aware of just how old a tradition was being continued.

Appendix 2
Folksongs referred to in text

Cod Banging

1. Come, come, my lads, and listen here.
   A fisherman's tale you soon shall hear.
   What I didn't undergo,
   When first I went a-cod-banging-o.

   Chorus: To my la-fol-de-day, riddle-all-day.
   This is a smacksman's life at sea.

2. How well I remember the fourteenth o' May.
   A big barque ship, she came our way.
   She came our way and she did let fly;
   And the tops'l halyards, they flew sky-high.

   Chorus

3. Now when we get to Harwich pier,
   The young and old they both draw near
   To see us get our fish on deck
   And crack their skulls with a bloody great stick.

   Chorus

4. And now my story's nearly done,
   I hope I've not offended one.
   I don't think that I've got it complete
   'Cause I've only been at sea for just about a week!

   Chorus

This traditional Essex song was released on the Topic folk label in 1973 and features on an album entitled *Songs from Suffolk* by Bob Hart, of Snape (1892-1978). Presumably, it is meant to be seen as the account of a comparative newcomer to fishing, with a delightfully ironic statement made in the last two lines of the fourth verse. Fish landed alive in the manner described here were caught on handlines and longlines, not in trawls, and killed on being landed by a sharp blow to the head. It was this lethal method of despatch which was referred to as *cod banging*. Hart himself had worked out of Lowestoft on a sailing smack in the years before the First World War, until a bout of pneumonia forced him to come ashore in 1912. Harwich and Lowestoft are quite some distance apart, but he had obviously come across the song by some means or other and made it part of his repertoire.

Gorleston Light

The farmer has his rent to pay.
Haul, you joskins, haul!
And seed to buy, I've heard him say.
Haul, you joskins, haul!
But we who plough the North Sea deep,
Though never sowing, always reap
The harvest that to all is free –
And Gorleston light is home for me.
Haul, haul, haul, haul, haul.
Oh haul, you joskins, haul!

This lyric has the ring of a capstan-song about it. The last two lines are sung more slowly than the rest, with a crescendo to suggest the physical effort involved in the work. The lighthouse referred to is of red brick construction and was built in 1878. It remains a prominent feature of Gorleston's quayside environment, standing close to the notorious bend in the river, west of the harbour mouth itself. The town was a Suffolk community for centuries, before becoming progressively integrated during the nineteenth and early twentieth century with its larger and dominant Norfolk neighbour, Great Yarmouth. This process never sat easily with many Gorlestonians and a number of its fishermen and beachmen were fully aware of their long-time separate identity – and keen to maintain it.

Sailing Over the Dogger Bank

1. Sailing over the Dogger Bank,
   Oh, wasn't it a treat.
   The wind a-blowin' about east-north-east,
   So we had to had to give her sheet.
   You ought to have seen us relish
   The wind a-blowin' free,
   On a passage from the Dogger Bank
   To Great Grimsby.

   Chorus: So watch her, stop her, we're proper juba-ju.
   Give her sheet and let her rip,
   We're the boys to bring her through.
   You ought to have seen us relish
   The wind a-blowin' free,
   On a passage from the Dogger Bank
   To Great Grimsby.

2. Our skipper's a Shanghai rooster,
   He's been in many a gaol.
   Our mate's a proper one for the beer,
   He'll drink it by the pail.
   The crew are the rakings and scrapings,
   The Devil wouldn't have 'em in Hell.
   They should have been shot, the whole damn lot,
   And a bloody good job as well!
   Chorus

3. Now we're the boys to make a row
   When we come home from sea.
   We get right drunk and roll on the floor
   And have us a jubilee.
   We get right drunk and get in a fight
   And roll all over the floor.
   And when the rent is all of it spent,
   We go back to sea for more!

   Chorus

There are other versions of this song, which perhaps dates from the time of the sailing-trawler fleets that worked the Dogger Bank during the second half of the nineteenth century. Great Grimsby was the earlier name of the port, as opposed to the village of Little Grimsby which lay inland and further to the south, near the town of Louth. It was the discovery of the Great Silver Pit fishing-ground (with its huge quantities of prime sole located there) in 1837, by William Sudds of Brixham, which established Grimsby's fortunes as a dominant centre of the English trawling industry. Sam Larner of Winterton, Norfolk, recorded the song as *The Dogger Bank* on the album *Now Is the Time for Fishing* (Folkways Records, 1961) and also gave a rendition of the first verse in Charles Parker's radio ballad *Singing the Fishing* (Argo label, 1968) – this, the third of a series of eight revolutionary programmes in all and broadcast on the BBC *Home Service* on 16 August 1960.

Haisboro' Light

1. As we were a-fishing off Haisboro' Light,
   Shooting and hauling and trawling all night.

   Chorus: In this windy old weather, stormy old weather,
   When the wind blow(s) we all pull together.

2. We sighted a herring, the king of the sea.
   He said, "Now, old skipper, you'll never catch me!"

   Chorus

3. We sighted a cod with his big, bulgy eye.
   He said, "Look, old skipper, your rig is too high."

   Chorus

4. We sighted a mackerel with his stripy back.
   He said, "Time, old skipper, to change your main tack."

   Chorus

5. We sighted a conger long as a mile.
   He said, "Wind's gone easterly; now you won't smile!"

   Chorus

6. We sighted a plaice with spots on his side.
He said, "Look, old skipper, these seas you won't ride."

Chorus

7. We thought what these fishes were saying was right.
So we hauled in our nets and made for the light.

Chorus

The lighthouse referred to above stands in the parish of Happisburgh, on the North Norfolk coast. It was built in 1790 and stands 85 feet high. It was decommissioned by Trinity House in 1987 and is now maintained by an independent trust, which secured its operation by Act of Parliament in 1990. It featured on national television during the 1990s in the BBC *Challenge Anneka* series, when it was painted from top to bottom in its characteristic red and white bands. Unfortunately, the wrong type of paint was used for a coastal environment and remedial action was later required. The name of the parish where the light is located is pronounced as "Haisborough", which is the spelling usually given to the offshore sandbank and which features here in abbreviated form in this particular version of the shanty. The tune commonly used would seem to be a variant of *Blow the Man Down*. Sam Larner, a local fisherman and folk-singer, recorded a version of the song which was issued some years after his death by the Topic label on an album entitled *A Garland for Sam* (1974). A variant of it, known as *Up Jumped a Herring*, dispenses with the first verse and begins with the title as its opening line. The verses which then follow can vary a good deal in both the species referred to and the rhymes used.

Windy Old Weather

1. Now up get the sole with his eyes on the side.
Says he to the skipper, "Let me be your guide."

Chorus: In this windy old weather, boys, how the sea roar.
Stormy old weather, boys. How the sea roar.

2. Now up get the codfish with his great old head.
   He jumped on the foredeck and casted the lead.
   Chorus

3. Now up get the herring, the king of the sea.
   And he sung out, "Old skipper, you'll never catch me!"
   Chorus

4. Now up get the mackerel with stripes on his back.
   Says he to the skipper, "You're on the wrong tack!"
   Chorus

5. Now up get the plaice with spots on his skin.
   Says he, "The bag's full, boys. Do you haul it in!"

   Chorus

6. Now up get the sprat, he's the smallest of all.
   Says he to the skipper, "All hands to the trawl!"
   Chorus

7. Now up get the shark with his eight rows of teeth.
   He jumped down the galley and ate the corned beef!

   Chorus: In this windy old weather, boys, how the sea roar.
   Windy old weather, boys; stormy old weather boys.
   When the wind blow, boys, we'll all go together!

This variant of *Haisboro' Light* is customarily sung to a similar tune, but one which also has a ring of *Hearts of Oak* about it. The delivery is less melodious and rolling in nature than its counterpart, with a rougher edge to it. Both songs can be traced back into the nineteenth century to a song commonly known as *The Fishes*, in which the men singing improvised freely on the species of fish referred to and made up their own rhyming verses as they went along. Lest it be thought that a question is being asked in the second line of verse 5, with an exclamation mark incorrectly replacing a question mark, the word "Do" in this case is the old English form of the imperative – and an order is being given.

Threescore and Ten

Chorus: Oh, it's threescore and ten boys and men were lost from Grimsby town.
From Yarmouth down to Scarborough many hundreds more were drowned.
In herring boats and trawlers and fishing smacks well,
They had to fight the bitter night and battle with the swell.

1. Methinks I see a host of them, spreading their sails a-lee,
   As down the Humber they do glide all bound for the cold North Sea.
   Methinks I see on each small craft a crew of hearts so brave,
   Going out to earn their daily bread upon the restless waves.

Chorus

2. Methinks I see them yet again as they leave the land behind,
   Casting their nets into the sea the herring shoals to find.
   Methinks I see them yet again and they're all on board all right,
   With their sails close-reefed, their decks scrubbed down and their side-lights burning bright.

Chorus

3. October's night brought such a sight, 'twas never seen before.
   There were mast and yards and broken spars all washed up on the shore.
   There was many a heart of sorrow, there was many a heart so brave;
   There was many a fine and likely lad who'd found a watery grave.

Chorus

The words for this song were composed by a Grimsby fisherman, William Delf, in memory of the loss of life caused by the gale of 8-9 February 1889 – which brings into question the reference to "October's night" in the third verse (presumably, it is an error which crept in at some point later). In general terms, the lyrics are a tribute to the North Sea fishermen lost in this particular storm by one of their own kind, but they were at the time produced as a latter-day broadside ballad aiming to raise funds for the bereaved families. Grimsby lost six vessels in the gale and Hull two.

The Smacksman (1)

1. Once I was schoolboy and I stayed at home with ease.
   Now I am a smacksman, I plough the raging seas.
   I thought I'd like seafaring life, but very soon I found
   That it wasn't all plain-sailing, boys, out on the fishing-grounds!

Chorus: Heave away, coil away; let's heave up the trawl.
   When we get our fish on board, we'll have another haul.
   It's straightway to the capstan, and then you'll hear us say,
   "If we don't go home tomorrow, boys, it'll be the very next day."

2. Now, when we get our fish on board, we have them all to gut.
   We stick them in baskets and down the ice-locker put.
   We ice them down, we size them, we ice them all quite well;
   We ice them and keep them as safely as an oyster in his shell.

Chorus

3. Now, when we get to market, we have our fish to sell.
   We put them up on the quayside and hope that we've done well.
   The little old boys all stand around, the buyers they come too.
   You know they're goin' to rob you and there's damn all you can do!

Chorus

Finale: Don't call us common fishermen any more;
   Don't call us common fishermen any more, any more.
   Fresh fish to you we bring,
   Don't call us a common thing.
   We're as good as them that work upon the shore!

The references to hauling the trawl are accurate of a smack's working-practice, with the steam capstan providing the motive force necessary (man-power before that) and the cook down in the rope-room, coiling the warp. The sizing and icing of the catch is well founded also, and so is the observation made in the last verse as to the presence of young lads on the fish market (the Lowestoft school-truancy officers always knew where to go to locate boys missing from the classroom!). This version of the song probably does originate from Lowestoft and many of the port's fishermen were firmly of the opinion that the fish merchants were always out to do them down. The term "common fisherman" is one encountered in nineteenth century sources from time to time, particularly where fishermen had transgressed in the eyes of the law and therefore feature in court records. It also had a social ring about it, whereby shore-based people (especially those in the lower echelons of the middle-class) considered themselves superior to men who went to sea. Perhaps the best-known version of this song is the one recorded by Sam Larner (1878-1965) of Winterton, in Norfolk – arguably, East Anglia's most esteemed maritime folk vocalist. It features on the album, *A Garland for Sam*, which has been referred to earlier.

The Smacksman (2)

1. Oh, once I was a schoolboy and lived at home with ease.
   But now I am a fishing lad who ploughs the raging seas.
   I thought I'd like seafaring life, but very soon I found
   It was not all plain sailing when we reached the fishing-grounds!

Chorus: It was heave away on the trawl-warp, boys, and let's heave up our trawl.
   For when we get our fish on board, we'll have another haul.
   So heave away on the trawl-warp, boys, and merrily heave away,
   For it's just as light when the moon shines bright as it is at break of day.

2. Oh, every night in winter, as regular as the clock,
   On goes sou'wester, deep-sea boots and oilskin smock.
   Then straight away to the capstan, boys, and merrily heave away,
   For it's just as light in the middle of the night as 'tis at break of day.

Chorus

3. Oh, when the eight weeks are over, hard up the tiller goes,
   Sou'-west by west for Yarmouth Roads with the big jib on her nose.
   And when we reach the pier-head, all the lassies they will say,
   "Here comes our jolly fishing-lad that's been so long away!"

Chorus

This version of the song was collected by John Leather, the Essex maritime writer, from his grandfather and it was a favourite with the Colne estuary fishermen. Some of these sailed at one time in the Great Yarmouth trawling-fleets during the late nineteenth century, which is probably how the song travelled south. Bob Malster has further pointed out how some of the Colne cutters were employed to convey catches from the fishing-grounds to Billingsgate market, which gives another feasible connection. The song is obviously connected with Great Yarmouth and the Dogger Bank trawling voyages, but the word *lassies* in the last verse would seem to be more Scottish in origin than East Anglian. Surely, it ought to have been *mawthers*! Perhaps the influence of the Scottish drifter-crews and shore personnel, who came down every year for the autumn herring-season, had already exercised an influence on local parlance – unless "lassies" was deemed more artistic in tone than other words used to describe young ladies.

The Female Cabin Boy

1. 'Tis of a pretty female, as you shall understand;
   She had a mind for roving into some foreign land.
   Attired in man's apparel, she boldly did appear
   And engaged her with a captain, to serve him for one year.

2. She engaged her with a captain, his cabin boy to be.
   The wind, it being in favour, they did soon put out to sea.
   The captain's lady was on board, her face lit up with joy
   That her husband had engaged for her so handsome a cabin boy.

3. His cheeks were like the red, red rose; his side-locks they did curl.
   The sailors used to laugh and say, "He looks just like girl!"
   But eating seaman's biscuits his colour did destroy
   And the waist did swell of pretty Nell, the female cabin boy!

4. One night among the sailors there was an awful row,
   As through the Bay of Biscay their gallant ship did plough.
   They tumbled from their hammocks, their rest it did destroy
   To hear the dreadful groaning of the female cabin boy.

5. The doctor ran with all his might, a-smiling at the fun.
   To think a sailor-boy could have a daughter or a son!
   "The child belongs to none of us!" the sailors, they did swear,
   And stuck to the declaration when a daughter she did bear.

6. Then said the captain to his wife, "My dear, I wish you joy.
   'Tis either you or I betrayed our handsome cabin boy!"
   Then each took up a bumper and drank success to trade
   And to the female cabin boy who was neither man nor maid!

There are a number of versions of this song, which is also known as *The Handsome Cabin Boy* and *The Pretty Cabin Boy*. It began life as a broadside ballad in c. 1730 and finished up as an accepted part of the English folk music canon. The number of performers who produced recorded versions of it during the 1950s and 60s looks like a who's who of British traditional folk: Ewan MacColl, Jeannie Robertson, A.L. Lloyd, Louis Killen, Martin Carthy and Cyril Tawney. Bob Hart of Snape (referred to earlier) and Walter Pardon of Knapton, Norfolk, also included it in their respective repertoires, and Kate Bush even produced a version in 1985 as the B-side to her single, *The Hounds of Love* – this being the title, also, of the eponymous album on which it first featured.

Lighthouse **score** at Lowestoft, with the lighthouse just visible top left. The **score** is one of the eleven that led down to the **Beach** or the **Grit**.

Scottish sailing drifters, or **fifies**, at Great Yarmouth c. 1900. They have a **lugsail** on a movable yard on the **mainmast**.

Postscript: the sinking of the *Eta*

Given the subject matter of Appendix 1, it has been thought relevant to include the following account of the loss of the diesel trawler *Eta* (LT 57), which trawled up a mine, on 5 January 1940, near the Outer Gabbard lightship off the Suffolk coast. This vessel was one of seven built by the Richards shipyard in Lowestoft, between 1933 and 1939, for a company called L.T. 1934 Ltd. Twelve boats were planned in all, but the outbreak of hostilities with Germany brought an end to the programme and it was not continued after the war. These small, near-water craft were very much an indicator of the way forward in fishing vessel development. Their compact design (they varied between 32 and 36 net tons) and Ruston-Hornsby engines (150 or 220 horse-power) made them efficient, and the comparatively low number of crew carried (six men) kept their operating costs down.

Edward John Mullender of Pakefield (1896-1981), universally known as "Ned", worked for L.T. 1934 Ltd. during the late 1930s and for the first few months of the Second World War. He was skipper of the *Eta* at the time of her sinking, but not on the fateful trip because of illness. His experience of the incident will now be recounted, in his own words, but no explanation is offered of what occurred. The reader must attempt to produce his or her own interpretation.

"I wuz in the *Eta*. She blew up. I wuz skipper o' the *Eta*, fishin' out here. This wuz the Christmas trip in thirty-nine, an' I went out an' got pneumonia. An', o' course, I went an' see the doctor when I come hoom, an' he ordered me straight t' bed, with kylon [kaolin] poultices an' all that sort o' stuff. Yeah. Poultices. They used t' put 'em on the chest.

"Now, the boat went t' sea agin on the Thursday. An' the Friday night I had this dream. I wuz in bed up here [indicating the bedroom above]. Now, all of a sudden, I wuz blew up. In the bed! I laid in my bed, but I think I'm on my ship. She wuz blew up, see. Now then, in the meantime, I said t' the boys, 'Now, look. She ent sinkin' fast. We're got time t' do everything.' We larnched the boat, an' she leaked, an' we pulled her back agin and wrapped a sail round her – the mizzen sail. We cut that adrift an' lashed it round the boat. See? 'Now,' I said, 'where are the oars?' The oars were blown out o' the boat, see, so we went an' got two shovels out o' the pound. An' I said t' the cook, 'Git my torch out o' my berth.' An' I hetta lower him down inta the cabin 'cause the steps were gone. All the port side stuff wuz down. That wuz a mine in the trawl, so they told me.

"Well, anyway, the cook – I lowered him down an' he got m' torch, an' he also got some o' my fags out o' my drawer. He wun't leave 'em. He come up wi' the torch, an' we got inta the little boat, an' we pulled away from her, an' I woke up. Wi' fright, see. An' my wife come inta the room an' say, 'Whatever is wrong wi' you?' She say, 'You're bin a-shoutin' an' gorn ahid.' 'Phew!' I say. I feel somethin' bad." She say, 'Oh?' She say, 'Whass up?' I say, 'I've hed a rotten dream, ol' dear.' She say, 'What about?' I say, 'My ship's blew up!' 'No!' she say. 'You're hed a nightmare.' I say, 'All right.' 'Cause I wuz too ill to argue, see.

"Well, o' course, about half-past nine in the mornin', up come my brother-in-law – my oldest brother-in-law, Bob Butcher. An' he say, 'How's the ol' boy?' My wife say, 'Oh, I dun't know.' She say, 'the doctor is comin' in agin t'day.' She say, 'He's gone delirious.' So he say, 'Oh?' 'Yis,' she say. He say, 'Is he fit t' hear the news?' She say, 'What news?' He say, 'His boat wuz blew up last night!' She say, 'What!' He say, 'His boat wuz blew up last night.' She say, 'What time?' He say, 'Oh, just afore dark.' 'Well,' she say, 'He wuz a-dreamin' that last night an' shoutin' all the odds.' She say, 'The crew are saved, 'cause he said so. They pulled away from the ship. They were in the little boat, paddlin' away wi' shovels.' 'Yeah,' he say. 'Thass what they say.' He say, 'The crew are all right, 'cause the crew are in.' See? One o' the other boats picked 'em up. So, anyway, he come up an' told me.

"Well, o' course, now, I'm another fortnight or three weeks afore I'm well. See? Well, after I got downstairs, away come the cook. Yeah, the cook what I lowered down, yuh see. He come up here an' knocked on the door. An', o' course, he wuz a big, tall boy. He wuz about six-foot-two. His nairme wuz Hood. I believe he become a window-cleaner or somethin'. An' he say t' me, 'I've brought your torch back, skipper.' He say, 'I dint give it t' anyone else.' He say, 'I kept it.' He say, 'I thought t' m'self: well, I'll go an' see the skipper.' Then he say, 'But I hent brought the fags back.' I say, 'What d' yuh mean?' He say, 'I took the cigarettes out o' your drawer, an' some matches.' He say, 'I thought t' m'self: I ent gorn t' let them sink!' See? I lowered him down [in the dream], but they lowered him down, really [on a rope]. Yeah, they lowered him down. He suggested it. He say t' one of 'em, he say, 'Let's git the skipper's torch.' Gus Durrant wuz skipper then. He wuz my mate an' he took her out, skipper. An' the third hand went mate.

"All the things I dreamt fell inta place aboard the boat. Everything I dreamt, thass what the boy told me had happened! Yeah, but I dreamt it about five or six hours later. Yeah, thass true. An' thass the reason I dun't like dreams. Several times my dreams ha' bin pretty close to true. I dun't have 'em very orften, but when I do I'm frightened if thass the wrong sort o' dream. O' course, if that ent – well, I dun't mind. But, as I said, everything fell in exac'ly."

Sailing drifters at Lowestoft fish market, circa 1900. On the right is the **lower landing** or **waling**..

Select Bibliography

Use of Language

Butcher, D., *Rigged for River and Sea* (Hull, 2008).
Claxton, A.O.D., *The Suffolk Dialect of the Twentieth Century* (Ipswich, 1954).
Forby, R., *The Vocabulary of East Anglia* (London, 1830; Newton Abbot, 1970).
Malster, R., *The Mardler's Companion: A Dialect Dictionary of East Anglian Dialect* (Ipswich, 1999).
Moor, E., *Suffolk Words and Phrases* (Woodbridge, 1823; Newton Abbot, 1970).
Nall, J.G., *An Etymological and Comparative Glossary of the Dialect and Provincialisms of East Anglia* (London, 1866).
Onions, C.T., *The Shorter Oxford English Dictionary* (3rd edition, 14th revision, Oxford, 1973).
Simpson, J.A., and Weiner, E.S.C., *The Oxford English Dictionary*, 20 vols. (2nd edition, Oxford, 1989).
Wright, J., *The English Dialect Dictionary*, 6 vols. (Oxford, 1898; Oxford, 1970).

Fishing, Marine Species and Varia

Benham, H., *The Codbangers* (Colchester, 1979).
Butcher, D., *The Driftermen* (Reading, 1979).
        The Trawlermen (Reading, 1980).
        Living from the Sea (Reading, 1982).
        Following the Fishing (Newton Abbot, 1987).

       The Ocean's Gift (Norwich, 1995).
Campbell, A.C., *The Hamlyn Guide to the Seashore and Shallow Seas of Britain and Europe* (London, 1976).
Davis, F.M., *An Account of the Fishing Gear of England and Wales* (London, 1923; London, 1958, 4th ed.).
De Caux, J.W., *The Herring and the Herring Fishery* (London, 1881).
Dyson, J., *Business in Great Waters* (London, 1977).
Elliott, C., *Sailing Fishermen in Old Photographs* (Reading, 1978).
       Steam Fishermen in Old Photographs (Reading, 1979).
Evans, G.E., *The Days That We Have Seen* (London, 1975).
Festing, S., *Fishermen* (Newton Abbot, 1977).
Finch, W., *The Sea in My Blood* (Weybread, 1992).
Frost, T., *From Tree to Sea* (Lavenham, 1985).
Gray, M., *The Fishing Industries of Scotland* (Oxford, 1978).
Griffin, S.C., *A Forgotten Revival* (Bromley, 1992).
Higgins, D., *The Beachmen* (Lavenham, 1987).
Hodgson, W.C., *The Herring and its Fishery* (London, 1957).
Leather, J., *The Northseamen* (Lavenham, 1971).
Lee, A.J., *The Directorate of Fisheries Research* (Lowestoft, 1992).
Lewis, C., *Pierhead Paintings* (Great Yarmouth, 1982).
Malster, R., *Saved from the Sea* (Lavenham, 1974).
       Maritime Norfolk, Part One (Cromer, 2012).
       Maritime Norfolk, Part Two (Cromer, 2013).
March, E., *Sailing Drifters* (London, 1952).
       Sailing Trawlers (London, 1953).
Mather, E.J., *Nor'ad of the Dogger* (London, 1887).
Muus, B.J. & Dahlstrøm, P., *Collins Guide to the Sea Fishes of Britain and North-Western Europe* (London, 1974).
Nall, J.G., *Great Yarmouth and Lowestoft* (London, 1866).
Oliver, R.C., *Trawlermen's Handbook* (London, 1965).
Smylie, M., *Herring* (Stroud, 2004).
Rose, J., & Parkin, D., *The Grit* (Lowestoft, 1997).
Starkey, D., et al. (eds.), *England's Sea Fisheries* (London, 2000).
Thompson, P., *Living the Fishing* (London, 1983).
Wheeler, A., *The Fishes of the British Isles and North West Europe* (London, 1969).

www.ingramcontent.com/pod-product-compliance
Lightning Source LLC
Chambersburg PA
CBHW070659100426
42735CB00039B/2326